DUKE NUKEM 3D™: UNAUTHORIZED GAME SECRETS

Michael van Mantgem & Kip Ward

D0108987

PRIMA PUBLISHING
Rocklin, California
(916) 632-4400

Project Editor: M. Scott Schrum
Developmental Editor: Michael Koch

Important:

ISBN: 0-7615-0783-3
Library of Congress Catalog Card Number: 96-68689
Printed in the United States of America

96 97 98 99 HH 10 9 8 7 6 5 4 3 2 1

DUKE TOC

Acknowledgments

As authors, we know we only wrote the words. By that we mean every member of the Prima team was responsible for creating this beautiful book. If we had our way, their names would grace the cover of this book along with ours.

Special thanks to Debra, Paula, Matt, Michael, and Brett for their belief in our abilities and their commitment to publishing incredibly high-quality books—without them this project would never have even been started. Thanks to Joe and Robert for their technical support. Big thanks to Scott and Andrew for transforming our pedantic words into golden prose. A tip of the pen is owed to Dan and Julianne for their marketing savvy. Thanks also to Victor, Mike, Lori, Vanessa, Kari and Kris for the truly breathtaking cover and interior, and for pulling all the pieces together to create a book.

Michael van Mantgem & Kip Ward
May 31, 1996

INTRODUCTION

Welcome to the third installment of the Duke Nukem saga. Gone are the days when Duke politely collected soda cans and happily scrolled across the screen like a crew cut-wearing cousin of the Mario Brothers. Happy happy, joy joy. After he made those bad aliens go away in *Duke Nukem™ 1 & 2*, he probably busted out his ABBA 8-tracks and hung out at the mall.

But Duke Nukem has grown into his name at last. He doesn't go to the mall anymore, and he's thrown away his teeny-bopper music. Let me introduce you to a tougher-n-nails action hero who gulps 'roids, loves the smell of napalm in the morning, and knows his way around America's most depraved strip joints. It's a good thing he's grown up—the aliens in *Duke Nukem 3D™* would yawn as they ground the younger, PC-Duke into a bloody pulp.

As the new and improved Duke Nukem, you must stop the extra-terrestrial horde from stealing the earth's women and transforming them into aliens. Prepare yourself for a Duke v. Aliens battle royale that Don King would die to promote. If the men of the world hadn't disappeared and its women weren't in cocoons, imagine the possibilities on pay-per-view.... But the stakes are much higher than simple market-share: if the aliens win, they'll take over the world—no more 4-wheelin', NRA meetings, Walmart, WWF, and Playboy. That's gotta hurt.

This situation should make you, the red-blooded action hero Duke Nukem, absolutely rage. The earth and its women are ours! In fact, you should probably throw down this book right now, break out the heavy weapons and deal death with a heavy hand. Right?!

Wrong. That's exactly what those aliens bastards are counting on you to do. Hmmmmm...best to do some recon before charging into battle.

With that said, it's my belief that any jarhead with an RPG can blast his way through this game. But it takes a thoughtful, more introspective Duke to explore and appreciate the nuances of this quest to save our chicks.

HOW TO USE THIS BOOK

If you've played any of the myriad *DOOM*™ games, *Duke Nukem 3D* will feel familiar. However, that doesn't mean you're in for a boring time. Quite the opposite is true—but you already know that, or you wouldn't have this book in front of you.

Duke Nukem 3D Unauthorized Game Secrets offers many types of help for Dukes of many different colors, besides red ('cause if you're red, you're dead).

Part One: Basic Training provides an overview of the *Duke Nukem 3D* arsenal, the monsters you fight, hard-earned battle tactics and dirty tricks, and a list of the divine and sublime *Duke Nukem 3D* cheat codes. Personally, I love cheats. In fact, I hate games where you can't cheat you're way through: being frustrated isn't fun. Games should be fun, and part of that fun is being able to chose when or not to cheat. Speaking of cheats, Part Two: The Blast Through is a cheaters paradise. You'll find:

- detailed maps of every mission—including the secret missions;

- a complete rundown of the items you'll find (and where); and,

- a by-the-numbers dash through of each mission, which pauses to reveal every secret area, unlock every puzzle, and comment on the more amusing sight-gags.

Part Three: The Nukem Network gives you an overview of *Duke Nukem 3D's* awesome network play capabilities, and finally, an appendix whets your appetite on how to best manipulate the built-in *Duke Nukem 3D* game editor. In other words, if you don't like what you see, or think you could do better, this section is for you. Real heavy-hitters, though, will want to check out Prima's *Duke Nukem 3D Construction Kit: Unauthorized*. How's that for a shameless plug?

Now that you know what to expect, it's time to get down and dirty. Forge ahead, Duke Boy, and let's show these alien scum-bags who's boss.

PART ONE
BASIC TRAINING

Like many other computer-based action games, the path you chose to victory is more of less up to you. Even so, there is a quasi-logical order of progression through each mission. With that said, the intent of each mission's walk-through in this book is to balance the antipodes of efficiency and enjoyment. In other words, stick with us and you'll encounter all the items, baddies, and built-in secrets—without tedious backtracking. Heck, we even let you in on some of the game's inside jokes. So not only will you exterminate those alien bastards, but you'll be in the know. What could be cooler than that?

CHAPTER 1
DUKIN' IT OUT IN THE ALIEN NATION

One of the first things you ought to do when you start playing *Duke Nukem 3D* is experiment with every difficulty setting. Chances are, if you're new to this genre of game you'll feel most comfortable on the easiest level. However, we wrote this book assuming you'll eventually play at the higher levels—so as you become more adept at the game, this book will continue to be useful to you. If you don't encounter some of the monsters or items specifically mentioned, then be a man and go get some! Moreover, the first time you encounter a new event, item, or monster, we take a few moments and go into some detail about it. Mercifully, our descriptions become lean and mean as we delve deeper in the game—which is just the way it ought to be. Now you know why the first missions may seem disproportionately long-winded.

With that said, winning a mission requires a delicate balance of raw firepower and cat-like finesse. It's one of those yin-yang type of thingys. Read on, Grasshopper Nukem. You may just achieve that balance.

WEAPONS

If you've flirted with any of the many *DOOM* games, Duke's weapon stock will strike you as suspiciously familiar. You kick baddies, shoot them, and blow them up. Fun. The slavishly similar weaponry in the *DOOM*-style games has to do with how the *DOOM* game engine computes ammo and hits, how the weapon is manipulated, and how those factors are integrated into game play. In fact, if you dig into Duke's built-in game editor, you can change or modify most everything except the weapons. In fact, to create new *Duke Nukem 3D* weapons (or to modify the present ones) means re-writing the entire game engine. Yuk.

Essentially, the very same program the staff at 3D Realms used to create *Duke Nukem 3D* is built right into your CD platter. Weapons aside, this means you can build *Duke Nukem 3D* levels literally from the ground up. You build your levels in 2-D, then get into the game and add textures and bad guys with the click of a mouse. The trick isn't creating a level; the trick is making the game play fun. Check out Prima's *Duke Nukem 3D Construction Kit: Unauthorized* for the complete scoop.

The game's built-in help function (dnhelp.exe) does an excellent job describing the vital statistics of each weapon. But what's really important is how they work in the heat of combat. Right? Read on. . . .

- Duke's mighty right foot. This is Duke's answer to DOOM's brass-knuckled fist. Luckily, you only have to rely on it at the beginning of Death Row—unless you're a bad Duke and cheat to give yourself everything. If you're in combat and it's the only weapon you have left, prepare to re-"boot" the game.

- Pistol. You'll probably carry around a full load of bullets because aliens like to cough these up when you smoke them. Consider this your last-gasp weapon in battle: each clip contains 12 rounds, and the gun takes forever to reload—which leaves you wide open to attacks. However, the pistol should be your weapon of choice for blowing open grates, urinals, fire hydrants, windows, buttons, and anything else that can't shoot back at you. From a distance, the pistol can be used to manipulate the various switches and buttons you'll come across.

- Shotgun. There's little doubt that this pump-action gun will quickly become your weapon of choice. The delay between rounds is faster than a pistol clip reload, and allows you a few seconds to turn and aim at your next target. In the hands of a skilled mass-(alien) murderer, it's like grooving to the rhythm of a primal drum. The shotgun's major limitation is range—like in real life, the farther away you are from your target, the less effective each blast is.

- Chaingun. I recommend using this weapon when you get stuck in a crowd of baddies—three or more enemies. However, this weapon gulps ammo! If you're not careful, you can easily spit out 200 rounds in a matter of seconds. When you use this gun, rely on controlled, short bursts. A box of ammo contains 50 rounds, but it doesn't seem to be enough. Like in DOOM, each chaingun round scores the same amount of damage as a pistol round. However, it's relentless rate of fire keeps enemies from getting the chance to fire on you—especially handy when you're low on health points.

- RPG. This is the baddest weapon in the game. This behaves exactly like the rocket launcher of DOOM fame. Use in combination with a Holoduke, as a single shot can turn an entire troop of baddies into bite-sized chunks. Yummy. The exceptions are the level bosses, where as many as 45 direct RPG hits are needed for victory.

- Pipebombs. This is the coolest weapon Duke's arsenal. As a kid, my friends and I built a few pipebombs, but nothing quite like these. Man. (For more details on effective pipebomb use, see Specific Tactics, below.)

Note

If you fire the RPG or detonate a pipebomb in a small area, you'll probably send Duke to the great beyond and need to restart the level. These are mighty powerful weapons, and if you respect them they'll respect you.

- Laser Tripbombs. The delayed action of the tripbomb gives an added dimension to death-dealing. Simply place the small plaque on any flat surface, and a few seconds later a red beam of light will shoot across to the facing wall. When the light beam is interrupted, a wicked explosion nails the transgressor.

- Freezethrower. The Freezethrower (or freezer) is an intriguing device, but it does come with some combat limitations. Namely, that your victims thaw out in a few seconds, and most targets take an appreciable amount of ammo (and thus time in combat) to immobilize. Also, you have to follow up your initial attack with some kind of shattering blow, requiring either that you fire on each target twice, or dart about wielding your shoe. Freezethrower projectiles do display a nifty ability to bounce off of almost any surface, and therein lies the greatest tactical advantage: enemies waiting around corners can be frozen if you know your angles.

- Shrinker. The Shrinker is sure to be a crowd favorite, though it has some of the same disadvantages as the Freezethrower in that the effect wears off after a brief time. Still, punks can be shrunk down rapidly, and since Duke's stomping is an automatic function, the actual death blow is easily delivered quickly to many small foes. The device's ability to shrink Assault Commanders makes it especially handy.

- Devastator. The high-end Duke weapon in terms of pure destructive capability, the Devastator is what you whip out when you don't care if they never find all the body parts. Ammo, of course, is relatively scarce, and a brief tug of the trigger rips through rounds faster than any other instrument of destruction. Use this baby on Boss Monsters, or to clear large areas of lesser losers before a counter-attack can be mustered.

THE STUFF OF LIFE

Snagging weapons and ammo to deal out death is only one aspect of Duke Nukem's journey of self-discovery. Generally speaking, if you see an item, grab it. The game's designers are very thoughtful gods, providing all the stuff Duke needs to survive when he needs it.

Every item has a limited and definable life-span (unless you're a god). Watch the inventory window carefully. A most unheroic way to die is to free fall due to a lack jet pack fuel (or to drown for a lack of oxygen; or to get a fatal dose of radioactivity because your boots failed). Staying alive in this hostile land means playing heads-up at all times. But be smart about grabbing goodies. If, for example, you already have scuba gear with 90 percent of its oxygen remaining and you stumble across another set of scuba gear, you might not want to grab it until you've depleted your current oxygen supply. Why? Because you can't have more than 100 percent of anything in this game, except for health points. In other words you only give yourself a measly 10 percent of oxygen. So why settle for 10 percent when you can get 100 percent? It's not unlike a race car driver who goes the extra lap before refueling: either he'll run out of gas before the pits, or he'll win the race. The point isn't to play *Duke Nukem 3D* exactly like your driving in the Indy 500. Simply play mean and lean and stretch your resources to their limits. Doing so is at times the only way to survive a mission without cheating or dying over and over again.

So, if you come across a large medkit and have 95 health points, what are you going to do? You're going to make a note of it and keep going because sometime later a lowlife alien will take you down a notch or two. . . .

DUKE'S CARRY-ON BAGGAGE

Greed is good and more is better. To grab an item all you have to do is walk over it. Score! To select an item, press one of the bracket key caps [] or [] , hit (Enter) to select your item, and (Enter) again to use it. You can also use the letter keys to make your selection; simply press its corresponding key cap (refer to the list below) and your item of choice is ready—if you have it.

☞ Portable medkit (key cap (M)). When you have it, hit the magic key for up to 100 health points. Ahhhh. Each portable medkit has 100 health points within it. In other words, if you're at 60 health and you heal yourself, you're in effect taking 40 health points out of this medkit. That means you'll have 60 health points still left in it. Bitchin'.

These are scarce to come by, so be smart and make each heal-up count. I suggest you allow your health run down to dangerous levels before you pump back up to normal—keep in mind the race car driver analogy mentioned above.

- Armor. It looks as good as it protects—so-so. When you wear it, you still take damage from enemy attacks, but at a lesser rate. And when it shreds, well. . . . On occasion, pig cops drop some after you've fried their bacon—and somehow the armor is always just your size.

- Jet pack (key cap [J]). This is he second coolest item in the game. In Episode One, you only really need it when you battle the final boss. In God Mode (besides being invincible) you get unlimited jet pack time. Way fun.

- Scuba gear. It's the underwater counterpart to the jet pack. If you master one, you'll master the other. Unlike the jet pack, Duke automatically dons the gear (if he has it) whenever he delves into the briny deep. Like in real life, your dive time is limited—unless you're a god.

- Nuclear boots. This is all that stops nuclear sludge ponds and lava flows from roasting you alive. These boots were made for wading; and lucky for you, Duke is smart enough to automatically put them on before splashing into the mire.

- Steroids (key cap [S]). They are similar to DOOM's Berserker Pack, but faster-acting. Once you down a bottle, you can't stop the effects. Moreover, its effects wear off once the counter runs down to zero. 'Roids are probably best used for making otherwise impossible leaps. It also makes Duke's Mighty Foot extra kicky. Zounds! Who needs a jet pack and a RPG? I'll tell you where to 'roid up in the walkthrough.

- Holoduke (key cap [H]). By far the coolest item in the game. Like pipebombs, only your imagination limits Holoduke's usefulness. In close combat, he's alien bait. In open areas, he's a campfire that Octobrains, Pig Cops, and regular Alien troopers love to swarm around. In essence, the bad guys gravitate toward the Duke who is closest to them. He appears where you activate him—

which means you have to actually dash into an area to drop him. But you can deactivate him from any distance.

- Night vision goggles (key cap N). When the world is dark, flip on these goggles and you will see! What's better, it lets you see monsters in a nifty glow-in-the-dark green—the same tint that plastic model kits of Godzilla, The Mummy, and Frankenstein that many red-blooded kids blew up in their youth. (See pipebombs, above.) In Deathmatch, the goggles allow you to determine if an enemy Duke is a Holoduke or not—obviously, a very cool feature.

Stuff Duke Encounters

Put it this way, if it would help, hurt, or even kill you in real life, it'll do the same to Duke.

- Medkits. These come in two sizes: Good and Better. They boost you to a maximum of 100 health points. The small medkits are tiny white boxes with red crosses and give you a maximum of 10 health points; the large ones give you a maximum of 30 points. See "Carry-on Baggage" for information on the portable medkit.

- Ammo. Guerrilla combat means being a smart scavenger. Even though you're Duke Nukem, you have a limit on the amount of ordnance you can carry. The menu bar at the bottom of the game screen shows you that limit. The table below lists what you'll find when you stumble across a given box of ammo:

Pistol clip	12 rounds
Shotgun box	10 shells
Chaingun magazine	50 rounds
RPG	5 rockets
Pipebomb box	5 bombs
Freezethrower	50 rounds
Devastator	50 shells
Shrinker	5 charges per crystal
Laser Tripbomb	Single units

- Healing Atoms. These always give you as many as 50 health points each—even if you're already topped out at 100— to a maximum of 200. Go out of your way to snag these gems.

- Trashcans. Shoot or kick them for junk inside. To open the plastic ones, you need to use a weapon that packs an explosive punch.

- Fire extinguishers. Think wall-mounted bomb. When you see one, stand back and shoot—especially before you investigate an area. Blowing one up enables you to drop an alien with a few pistol shots or a lurking pig cop with a single shotgun blast.

- High-pressure gas canisters. Think of these mathematically as fire extinguishers cubed. Stand clear and shoot. If you're lucky, a pig cop or alien will be standing nearby. Messy.

- Grate. Kick or shoot them out. Then crawl in and follow your nose.

- Card key lock. They come in three flavors: Yellow, Red, and Blue. All you have to do is match the proper color key with its corresponding lock. The trick isn't in opening the lock, but in finding the key.

- Button lock and switches. At times there is only a single button or switch to punch with your [Spacebar]. The Button Locks can also be activated with a bullet shot. You'll have to activate Button Locks with a bullet in the chapel of Episode One's Death Row, and toward the end of the Toxic Dump mission in the same episode.

  At other times, you'll be confronted with a row of buttons that must be depressed to open or unlock a door. In this book, the bold stars indicate which buttons must be turned on (a green light), and unbolded stars the ones that must be red (turned off), e.g. *** * ***.

- Big door. I shouldn't have to say this, but when you open a door, expect a monster to be laying in wait for you. You open a door by facing it and pressing the [Spacebar]. Simple. Some doors are locked with a color-coded lock, and to unlock the door you need its corresponding colored key. Other doors have button locks. They can be a single button (shaped like a hand), or a series of buttons that are, in effect, a combination lock.

☞ Little door. These conceal keys and other special items. Unlike their big counterparts, you only need to hit [Spacebar] to open them.

☞ Sliding panel/wall/poster. These usually conceal hidden or secret areas and only require you hit the [Spacebar] to open them. Once you've cleared a room of bad guys, you can either go around an entire room hitting the [Spacebar] or find it by reading the walkthrough. The choice is yours.

☞ False wall/window/waterfall. This usually takes hours to find—unless you have this book—and they usually conceal a secret area. One way to find a false door, wall, or window is to fire a rocket at what looks like a solid wall or window. If the projectile explodes on the surface, it's solid. If it disappears, you've hit your mark. That's exactly how I found these secret areas. Needless to say, it required a countless number of rockets and hours of jet pack time; but if you wanted to find them on your own, why did you buy this book? Unlike me, you have better things to do with your time.

☞ Lift/elevator. Usually all you have to do is step in (or on) and hit the [Spacebar]. Other times you'll have to shoot a button. Not surprisingly, there's usually an alien waiting for you at the end of your ride. So, if you think a bad guy is waiting for you, why not foreshadow your grand entrance with a Holoduke and pipebomb treat? Just toss one in, drop Holoduke, stand on the edge of the lift's entrance, and hit the [Spacebar]. Surprise! This is also a great Dukematch strategy.

☞ Puckered wall. A single, well-placed RPG shot or pipebomb blows a hole in the wall—that is exactly what you're supposed to do. Once you're familiar with how they look, you'll never miss one. I point out each one as they're encountered in the mission walkthroughs.

- Mirror. Besides giving you the ability to double check your hairdo, you should use the mirrors to spy on any aliens before you swoop into an area, guns blazing. It's a very, very cool game feature.

- Urinals, commodes, fire hydrants, and the healing power of water. Though Duke hates playing with fire, he loves water sports. Approach any urinal or commode and hit the (Spacebar)—not only does this spell relief, but, once per mission, you get 10 free health points. Then blow them open (including fire hydrants), stand in the fountain, and hold down (Spacebar) and watch Duke's health creep up one point at a time, maxing out at 100.

- Monitor. You come across a security monitor now and again. Hit the (Spacebar) to activate it. Keep pressing the (Spacebar) to toggle through each of the camera stations. Essentially, they show you where you're going and where you've been. When you're playing against the monsters, you shouldn't need to use them. Hey, you're already proactive and bought this book!

  But when you're playing Dukematch—suffice to say that these are invaluable recon tools. Not only can you locate your adversaries, but watch them walk right into any traps you may have set. Conversely, be aware of where the cameras are located—and smile, you're on Dukematch Camera.

- Shrink rays. This is "getting small" the easy (and legal) way. You won't take any damage when you shrink, and the effect only lasts a few seconds (usually just enough to get you through a small passage). If you suddenly get big where you ought to be small, say good-bye to this life and restart the mission—you're dead.

  Shrinking monsters is way cool—when they're small, all you have to do is go up next to them. Duke automatically looks down and squishes them. Cool. Of course the bug can be on the other foot—when you're small, you're all but helpless. Just remember that "small people got no reason to live." (Hats off to Randy Newman's hit song that everyone loved to hate.)

- Laser Tripbomb. These are really wall-mounted bombs, and simply put, they'll fry your ass. If you trip one (and live) or a monster trips one, it explodes. The explosion will knock it out for good. Use pipebombs and RPG blasts instead of your body to knock them out. But there's a better way: with a little practice you can jump over or duck under most of them. When you encounter one, save your game and give it a try. When you encounter a wall of them, you have no choice but to stand back and blow them up real good. If you're lucky you can draw a baddie into the deadly beam, but don't bet your life on it.

☞ Teleporter. They work just as you'd expect. Just step in and go! If you've played *DOOM* or watched *Star Trek*, you've already seen these in action. Most of them go two ways, so you can usually go back from where you came.

☞ Gears/moving platform. They are an extremely cool feature. You get to jump on top of them or go between them. And if you mis-time your jump or entrance, you'll be squashed like a bug. Game over. Though I can't teach you keyboard dexterity, I will lend some hard-earned advice: TURN OFF GOD MODE AND SAVE YOUR GAME BEFORE YOU LEAP. If you slip up (and you will) and God Mode is on, you'll be crushed in a time loop of never-ending death and never-ending life. The only way out of this existential dilemma is to reboot. Many Duke Nukems were sacrificed in order to bring you this information.

☞ End mission nuke badges. Blast away the protective glass (if there is any) and hit the [Spacebar] to end a mission. I suggest you save your game before you finish a mission.

☞ Fire. If you play with fire, you'll get more than your fingers burned. The heavy breathing is your clue that Duke is smokin', so to speak. Yeeouch! Stay away from it, unless noted in the walkthrough.

☞ Nuclear sludge and lava. Here are two great tastes that taste great together. In stagnant pools both are deadly. In rivers, both are fast moving and deadly. Stay out of them as much as possible—even if you're wearing your protective boots. Proof once again that nothing (including nuclear-resistant footwear) lasts forever.

ALIEN BASTARDS

They're all so bad they need killing. Briefly, here's what you're up against.

REGULAR BAD GUYS

- Aliens. They are your basic shotgun fodder. In fact, a single shotgun blast is ruthlessly effective against these green meanies. They do pack a powerful laser attack and they fly via jet pack. If you're cocky or out of ammo, they can kill you quite easily. When you kill them they sometimes drop pistol ammo. Oh boy.

- Alien Lieutenants. These are aliens of a different color—orange, to be exact. Other then their cheery uniform, they differ from the greenies in that they can teleport (usually behind you). When you hear one teleport, hit the Backspace key and get ready to fire.

- Pig Cops. These are LA cops taken over by aliens. Uh-huh. Sure. More importantly, they each carry a shotgun and go into a bloodthirsty frenzy if you come anywhere near them. But anyway you slice them, with your speed and combat savvy they're not much more than the other white meat. What's better, when a Pig Cop dies he may drop some armor and his weapon. If he drops his gun he'll be leaving you anywhere from one to four shells—depending on how many he's already fired.

- Pig Cop Recon Vehicle. The winged Pig Cop can be a serious threat, so clip those wings as quick as possible to bring the swine down to earth. The shotgun and chaingun prove particularly effective.

- Octabrains. Three shotgun blasts flattens them; a single RPG shot makes seared octo-sushi. They attack you with powerful mind blasts, which can be dodged if you're at a distance, and have a nasty bite. In other words, it's best to keep your distance. They especially love to gather around Holoduke, which makes for a touching Boy Scout-like campfire scene. A tear never fails to cloud this Scoutmaster's eye when I aim my RPG.

- Sharks. These fish are fast, but that's about all they have going for them. Attack from the same relative depth, and you won't have any trouble shotgunning them into submission.

- Protozoid Slimers. The pods spread about the second and third episodes are the Alien-esque embryos of the Protozoid Slimer. If at all possible, blast the pods before they have a chance to issue forth a slimy spawn. The Slimer itself is more bothersome than dangerous, but they can be hard to target as they jump from ceiling to floor. The chaingun works particularly well in splattering them with a minimal of aiming required.

- Sentry Drones. The suicidal Sentry Drone needs to be dealt with quickly, and from a distance. Drones dodge large projectiles, and pay Holoduke no mind, so whip out that chaingun or shotgun to detonate them from afar.

- Enforcers. The chaingunning footsoldier of the otherworld horde, Enforcers can present a problem in bunches. Their leaping also makes them difficult targets, so get used to the idea of leading them a bit. Should an Enforcer get the drop on you, expect to be slimed, a disorienting as well as damaging occurrence. Most drop chaingun ammo or a chaingun itself upon their timely demise.

- Assault Commanders. Floating in their hovercars, the Assault Commanders are bloated badasses with a serious Achilies heel. Though a Commander can tear you limb from limb with just a few missiles, he'll opt for a more personal attack at close range: kind of a spinning slap fight. And at close range they can easily be shrunk and stomped. Avoid sucking down incoming missiles, and close the gap. Shrink. Stomp. Next, please...

- Boss Monsters. So named due to their resemblance to the monster at the end of Episode One, the Boss Monster is formidable, but not nearly as unbeatable as the original. Less than 10 RPG shots send him packing, and there are also several opportunities in the game to kill a disadvantaged boss by lesser means. Use their inability to reposition the machine gun against them, by confronting them from above or while the beast is stopped in a doorway. usually, you can get in your licks without taking much grief in return.

- Turrets. These are deadly accurate opponents. It takes them about about five seconds to get wise to your presence once you enter their sphere of influence—just enough time to aim and launch an RPG shot. If were only that easy . . . they're usually accompanied by a host of baddies, often time putting you in the middle of a nasty crossfire. Because of their relentless fire, I recommend you take these out as soon as you can.

BOSSES

- Episode One boss: he's big and bad. He runs as fast as you. He wields a huge chain gun and unleashes an unholy barrage of grenades. It takes the equivalent of 45 RPG shots and all your tactical savvy to vanquish this monster. Good luck, Duke. Consider all the monsters in the first level as practice for the final showdown with this bad-tempered dude.

- Episode Two boss: this missile-toting toad is a serious challenge, especially if you find yourself low on Devastator ammo. Ducking into the chamber that the monster originates from can buy you time and supplies: not only do goodies lie inside that room, but coming back out again opens a secret door across the battle chamber, stocked with more supplies.

- Episode Three boss: the King Freak from another world is pure hell on Earth, a foe so deadly and quick that only Duke Nukem may live to tell the tale. Blow the blimp above the field to shower the area with weapons, ammo and health boosts, and try strafing with your RPG along the diagonal of the field. Afterward, well.... Here's proof that real men don't always go for the two-point conversion.

CHAPTER 2

GAME BASICS AND ATOM-SMASHING TIPS

We've touched on the weapons, items, and bad guys in this game. Now it's time to bring them all together. Some of the basics are:

- Get comfortable with the Run Mode. Use it at all times. Just make sure the [Caps Lock] key is depressed.

- Make strafing second nature. This means pressing the [Alt] key in conjuction with your arrow keys, thus allowing you to move laterally while you fire.

- Get comfortable with the [Backspace] key. Practice quickly and unpredictably changing direction and firing while you run backward. Remember, you can run just as fast in reverse as you can forward, but you can't fire behind your back.

- Use the crosshairs function. It's not cheating you're a high-tech warrior. Now, walking through walls and playing in God Mode . . . that's cheating.

- Learn how to duck, jump, and use walls and other barriers for cover.

Since we can't show you what we're talking about with a video clip, we suggest you take a look at the action going on behind the "Select a Game" introduction screen. The Duke in action is very quick and gutsy, even if he is a poor shot. Still, his smoothness and control when maneuvering around corners; his battlefield awareness that keeps the enemy in front of him; his outright opportunism; and the way he exploits his surroundings demonstrates the finer points of combat the Duke Nukem way.

GENERAL ATOM-SMASHING TIPS

In *Duke Nukem 3D*, seeing monsters doesn't necessarily mean you can kill them: you have to trigger them into action. Since you're faster and smarter than your enemy (and dare we say a super-genius for getting this book), go ahead and use a little psychology on them. Instead of slugging it out toe to toe, Rocky-style, jump out from behind a wall or into a room (and use your Holoduke if you can), jump back and wait for them to come to you. Your body is the best bait going. Be patient and lure them into your trap. When you're playing Aqua Duke, popping to the surface or dropping below the waves is similar to rounding a corner or opening a door. Expect monsters to attack. Remember tactics don't change, only the immediate situation does.

We suggest you save the game often, especially before you open a door or attempt to leap on or between gears. Moreover, we recommend you save before completing a mission. This way you can go back and mop up anything you may have missed (though you should have cleaned up if you were paying attention) and have a fresh start for the following mission time and time again. Or to put it another way, once you progress to a new mission, you can't go back.

OFFENSIVE TACTICS

What follows is some tactical advice:

- ⮞ Doors. It doesn't take genius to figure out that a bad guy probably lurks behind each door. In fact, let's call it the "Golden Rule of *Duke Nukem 3D*." As a good Nuke Scout, always be prepared.

Try to lure bad guys into closing doors. When the bad guys get squished, the door is transformed into a gory taffy-pulling machine. Try it and you'll see what we mean. Even if you can't squish them, go through an open door to stir up the bad guys and dash out the way you entered. If you keep them in eyesight, they fall prey to their most basic instinct and follow you. We've found that good ol' Holoduke makes a fine leave-behind tool in these situations. Drop him near the door to distract your enemies, haul-ass to a safe distance, and start blasting.

- Corners. Always assume a monster is lurking around one. Leap out and pop off a few caps, drop a Holoduke in the intersection if necessary, and leap back. You're much faster than any enemy you encounter and a veritable Einstein by comparison. Make them come to you (or Holoduke) and let them feel your pain.... 'Nuff said.

- Elevators & lifts. Like that old war tune, you never know where you're going 'til you get there. To preempt an underhanded alien attack, drop a Holoduke on a pipebomb and send this odd couple for a ride. The Holoduke should lure any nearby bad guys to the lift, and the bomb will surely blow them away. Bring the lift back, get out your favorite gun, and go see what sort of mess you made.

- Ledges. Practice walking and running on ledges in the earliest missions. Early on, you'll only take a few points of damage, at most, if you slip off. If you slip in later missions, you'll die. Ledges usually give you a tremendous height advantage. Use it.

- Open areas. You're a sitting Duke when you're out in open terrain. The only things between you and death are your running speed and combat savvy; but you don't have to go it alone. Open areas are a great place to put Holoduke to work. When you get outside, drop a Holoduke and run like hell. The monsters will fixate on it, giving you the luxury to dispense frontier justice from a distance. Moreover, you should always use the Run Mode in open areas (either underwater or on dry ground).

When in open areas underwater, we recommend using RPG blasts or pipebombs to waste the bad guys. The more quickly you kill them, the better. When you're underwater, oxygen is more valuable than ordnance—if you run out of air, you're dead; if you run out of ammo you can always bravely turn tail and flee.

Pipebombs. The longer you hold down the [Ctrl] key, the farther Duke tosses the bombs. If you're kneeling (by pressing [Z]) when you toss it, it only goes a short distance. You can toss them out of vent shafts, lob them over bathroom stalls or onto ledges above you, set boobytraps, go fishin' for Octobrains . . . your only limitation is your creativity. To throw multiple pipebombs, press [6] instead of [Ctrl] when the trigger button is up. Another pipebomb appears. Press [Ctrl] again to toss it. Repeat the process until you sufficiently saturate an area with them. As a bonus, on any given level, you can set your pipebombs off no matter where they are in relation to you. This is a nasty, way low-down, dastardly Dukematch trick. Skip ahead to Chapter 7 for details. Heh, heh.

Ducking and strafing. Besides climbing and running, Duke can duck and strafe. Duck behind window sills, pop up for a short burst of fire, and duck back down. Leap into a room, snap off a few rounds, and immediately dive for cover—most likely the bad guys will come to you. Above all else, be creative and use the cover "God" (a.k.a. the game designers) gave you.

Hunting and gathering. Simply put: economize. If, for example, you come across a box of RPGs and already have 49 (of a maximum 50), stepping on a box yields a measly one round. It's better to use up at least five rounds before you step on that box. Thrifty use of resources is especially important when you're battling the final boss at the end of Episode One.

Run don't walk. Depress the [Caps Lock] key to leave it on, or press the [Shift] key for a quick dash. Go dogface, go! Once you get used to running, you'll never walk again. In fact, the Run Mode is the only way to save your own hide in open areas and in later missions, where the general axiom is run or die. After all, only a nobody walks in L.A.

- Never forget you can run just as fast backward as forward. If you're getting blasted from behind, start running ([Caps Lock]), hit the [Backspace] key to instantly flip around, and start blasting as you double-time it in reverse. The distance gives you a chance to evade the alien shots and provides the split second breather you need to get your bearings.

- Fight from high ground whenever possible. Why do you think castles are built on hills and aliens have built-in jet packs?

- Jump off ledges and over your enemies. But don't stop there—in midair, hit [Backspace]. You'll do a clean 180° turn and land in time to maybe pump a round or two into your foes before they can respond. Jean-Claude would be proud.

- Watch the floor for shadows. When you see a shadow you can bet there's an alien in the sky who's just hanging around waiting to attack you. You can destroy this floater by detonating a pipebomb on its shadow. What a mess!

- Go into God Mode if you think you may run out of jet pack juice or oxygen. Doing so gives you unlimited jet pack and dive time. In this respect, cheaters always win.

DEFENSIVE TACTICS

Simply put: Get a good offense.

SWIMMING WITH THE OCTABRAINS

You'll do a lot of this, so it's worth some extra discussion. Swimming is dangerous in many ways: your oxygen reserve is limited—meaning if you're not careful you'll drown; if you swim in heavy water, you take damage (Duke's heavy breathing is your clue to when you're swimming in Three Mile Island Iced Tea); and, you can (and will) be attacked while you're still at the surface—the one place you can't fight back. What's our advice?

- ☞ Watch your dive time clock and conserve your oxygen supply. Your cause will be greatly helped if you keep Run Mode on at all times. Don't forget the race car driver metaphor, either!

- ☞ It's smart to avoid playing in heavy water.

- ☞ Stay out of the water unless you plan on diving in—and remember, there are no lifeguards on duty.

Here's a cool trick to try before you go into uncharted waters. Quickly jump in the drink, survey the area for monsters and use your body as a lure (or bait them with a Holoduke), get out and soften the water with a few pipebombs. It's just like fishing with dynamite. A similar pipebomb technique works with sludge and lava rivers. You're upstream, the monsters are down stream. . . . Suffice to say that timing is everything.

CHAPTER 3
SUREFIRE CHEATS

After a few missions, you've undoubtedly learned the hard way that those alien maggots play some serious hardball. If there was just some way to level the battlefield . . . after all, when the earth and its chicks are at stake, anything goes.

Any time during game play just punch in the cheat you want and BLAMMO! it's yours. No fuss, no mess. Know them, use them, live them, love them.

CODE	WHAT IT DOES	MESSAGE
dncornholio dnkroz	God Mode	"God Mode On/Off"
dnstuff	Gives you all items, weapons, and ammo	"Giving Everything"
dnitems	Gives you all non-weapon items	"Giving Everything"
dnweapons	Gives you all weapons	"Got all weapons/ammo"
dnclip	Turns clipping mode on and off, enabling you to walk through walls	"Clipping Mode Off"
dnscotty###	Lets you warp to you level of choice.*	-
dnskill#	Changes skill level to # (any number from 1 to 5)	-
dnview	Puts Duke in Chase Mode (same as F7)	-
dnhyper	Gives you steroids on demand	-
dncashman	Duke spews cash as long as you press Spacebar	-
dnmonster	Makes the monsters disappear— great for when you're going for time	-
dnshowmap	Provides complete mission map	-
dnrate	Show frame rate on top right of screen	-
dnbeta	Displays "Pirates Suck!"	-
dnallen	Displays "Buy Major Striker" (an Apogee game)	-
dncosmo	Displays "Register Cosmo Today!" (an Apogee game)	-

*The first # is for your episode choice, the second # for mission. E.g., Red Light District (Episode One, Mission 2) would be: dnscotty102

OK, the boring academic stuff is finally over. Now stick with us through the mission walk-throughs and you won't even muss up your crew cut. How's that for looking good?

PART TWO
THE
BLAST-THROUGH

CHAPTER 4

EPISODE ONE
L.A. MELTDOWN

Your quest begins with a blood-soaked stroll down the Walk of Fame and sorties into Hollyweird's "hottest" adult entertainment venues. What's worse, if the Aliens keep stealing our chicks, there won't be any left to star in the skin-flicks.... So what are you waiting for?

Unfortunately, the California dreamin' comes to an abrupt end after the second mission—where you find yourself stripped of all weapons and strapped to *Duke Nukem 3D's* version of Old Sparky. Yeeouch! It's proof that there *can* be too much barbecue, especially if you're what's for dinner. Relying on your brains, brawn, guts, and this book, you must fight your way out of Death Row, survive the destruction of a sabotaged submarine—and, of course, exact some revenge on the Alien horde.

Next you'll be baptized in pools and rivers of slime and fire as you quest to commandeer an Alien ship. Along the way, you can take a side trip to implode an Apollo 13-style rocket and fry some bacon. Cool.

Now that you know what's in store for you, follow along closely because the time has come to make those Alien bastards pay!

MISSION 1:
HOLLYWOOD HOLOCAUST

You didn't buy this book so we could pontificate on All Things Nukem. Through practice you'll learn how and when to run, turn right and left, jump up, or duck. Unless we miss our guess, you probably bought this book for the maps that detail the secret places. Hell, that's why we'd buy this book.

However, in this first mission description we went ahead and included the lurid details for the rookies out there—we don't want to lose any Dukes the first day out. Think of this particular walk-through as a first date—it introduces you to every core element in the game (weapons, items, monsters, jumping, flying, drinking, urinating, etc.)—that is, it quickly and cleanly sketches out the basics of Duke's world.

In the following missions we hone our focus on the difficult scenarios and culturally challenging stuff. Promise.

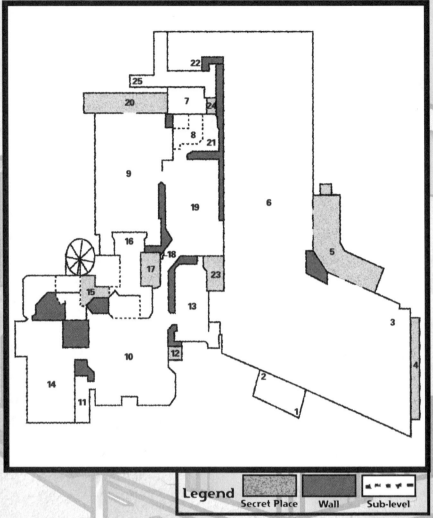

HIGHLIGHTS

- All eight secret places
- All six basic weapons—without using any cheats
- All four non-weapon items available on this level

MISSION 1: HOLLYWOOD HOLOCAUST AT-A-GLANCE

  1 Start, Pistol ammo
  2 Pistol ammo, medkit
  3 Medkit
* **4** RPG
* **5** Rockets, steroids, monitor
  6 Pistol ammo, Healing Atom, fire hydrant
  7 Medkit
  8 Alien
  9 Armor, pistol ammo, medkit
10 Switch (opens 12), Healing Atom, medkit, pistol ammo
11 Shotgun, medkit
***12** Armor
13 Pistol & ammo, medkit, monitor
14 Pistol, shotgun ammo, portable medkit, Holoduke
***15** Pistol ammo, shotgun ammo, monitor
16 Healing atom, red key, pistol ammo, medkit, steroids
***17** RPG
18 Night vision goggles, pipebombs, medkit
19 Pistol ammo, Holoduke
***20** Jet pack, shotgun ammo, monitor
21 Medkit, shotgun ammo
22 Ledge (shoot Pig Cops at 25 from here)
***23** RPG, chaingun, pipebombs, shotgun
***24** Turrets, jet pack, shotgun ammo
25 End

    *Denotes secret place

Blood & Guts in Tinseltown

1   Start. Step behind the nearby crate and pick up the ammo clip.

2   Shoot the fan (or the gas canisters: they blow up real good *and* dispose of the fan). Jump down the ventilation shaft. You take a few points of damage but you also land next to a medkit.

3   Blast the baddie off the box. Watch your back and jump on the box. This is a pivot point to two secret places! Jump to the angled ledge, then turn to face the street and leap onto the ledge to your left.

4   Secret place. You trigger the secret place by hugging the wall. Go forward and a platform will rise and offer up an RPG. You've probably been shot in the back a few times by now, so deal some death. Lob a rocket into the middle window on the lowest floor of the nearby building. Guess where you're going next?

> ### Note!
> The *Innocent?* on the billboard refers to the verdict of the O.J. Simpson trial. If you don't know about the event *that is* O.J., what have you been doing—playing computer games instead of watching *Court TV*? Shame on you.

5   Secret place. Go ahead, jump through the window and onto a glob of Alien. Now aren't you glad you fired that rocket? The "Secret Place" message appears just before you round the corner. Watch out for the Alien ambush! Hit the movie poster to reveal another secret place and a stash of 'roids. Jump out any of the windows, onto a ledge and to the ground. You'll take damage if you jump to the street directly.

6   There's lots to see and do in Hollywood. Rather than herd you down my favorite path, We'll let you explore these mean streets on your own. Beware that Aliens will appear out of thin air!

- Box office. If you shoot into the box office at about a 45-degree angle, you'll take out the Pig Cop waiting to punch you ticket, and open up a hole in the wall.

- Palm tree. You can hug the tree, but don't defoliate it with a rocket attack! You'll need to use the tree later.

- Dumpster. There's some smokin' hot pistol ammo in there.

- Street sign. It may be razor thin, but Duke *can* jump onto it. From there, leap to the ledge enroute to a Healing Atom on the left.

- Fire hydrant. Contains water—the urban elixir. If only Duke could pee on it . . . .

- Healing Atom. On the far-ledge across from the fire hydrant.

7   On the higher difficulty settings you'll be ambushed by two Pig Cops. Lure them out into the street to slaughter them on *your* terms. The window located to the right of the door looks into (20)—a secret room. You can smoke this dude from here or wait 'til later and use him for pipebomb practice.

8   On the higher difficulty settings, an Alien waits in ambush. Make that fire extinguisher on the far wall work for you by detonating it with a couple of pistol shots!

9   Wax the Aliens, grab the ammo, and snag the armor on the far end of the stage. Watch for Aliens lurking between the rows of seats. Fire an RPG shot into the projection booth. You're going up there soon enough, so why not soften it up? Exit the theater through either open door. Shake it baby. Battle your way toward (10) to dance with the Aliens.

10 Clear the room and jump over the counter. Watch your back for flying Aliens! Hit the cash register to reveal a secret room (12)—it's to your upper right as you face the register. Getting there is easier than you think—we'll do that in a minute. First, let's get some heavier firepower. Turn left as you face the register, and open the door at that end of the counter. A shotgun is on your right and the enemy on your left.

11 Do your business fast. Entering this room blows open the far wall at the other end of the counter, and bad guys issue forth. Inside the revealed area is a Healing Atom.

12 Secret place. Stand below the right edge of the alcove. Hit the [Spacebar] and ride a small platform up. It's hard to find this lift, but trust me, it's there.

13 You could have entered this room through (6) by blasting the wall out of the box office. If not, you still have an Alien and a Pig Cop (on the higher levels) to fight. Grab the stuff and let's go do some smokin' in the boy's room.

14 Wax the Alien perverts and snatch the shotgun ammo stashed behind the couch. Dethrone the Alien in the right-side stall. Take a leak, then blast out the bathroom fixtures to lap up the toilet water (if you can use the health points). Bad dog.

> **Note!**
>
> Look closely at the wall above the left urinal. You'll see the number 867-5309. If you're an old cur like me, you'll remember a one-hit wonder of the early 1980s by the name of Tommy Tutone. His hit song was *867-5309 (Jenny)*. For those who don't recall this musical masterpiece, it was a song about a guy who found Jenny's number on a bathroom wall and relentlessly harassed her.

Blast the grate above the toilet stalls, then follow that shot up with an RPG blast into the shaft. Grab the portable med-kit in the left alcove before you leap into the vent shaft. Grab the Holoduke inside the shaft and shoot out the next grate as soon as you see it.

15 Secret place. You can take out most of the Aliens from the vent shaft. If you didn't try to speak to the cocooned woman, go up to her and press the [Spacebar]. Do as she wishes, then slip just around the corner and hit the [Spacebar].

16 Welcome to the projection room. Down the baddies, grab the red key, ammo, and the 'roids. Hit the wall switch next

to the projection window. Oo-la-la! See how the screen is puckered up, so to speak? Nail the screen with an RPG shot, opening a way into (20). We'll go there momentarily. Get your shotgun ready and leap onto the top of the projector to open (17).

17 Secret place. Aliens and an RPG await. Fight your way down the circular stairway back to (10). Grab the medkit hidden in the alcove that appears after the earthquake.

18 Push the trashcan with the [Spacebar]. Jump on it, then jump straight up for pipebombs and night vision goggles. Activate the arcade elevator, wax the Alien that descends, and ride up.

19 Take out the Pig Cop, blast the yellow gas canisters, and quickly jump back into the elevator to avoid taking any damage. The resultant explosions will clear the room. Go to the *Duke Nukem* game, and hit the [Spacebar] for a great one-liner. A Holoduke is revealed in the wall to your right, but only for a moment: Grab it quick! Jump down through the hole the canisters created, and go to the theater screen.

20 Secret place. Toss in a few pipebombs, leap in to stir up the Aliens, leap out, and detonate. What a mess! Go back in for shotgun ammo and a jet pack. If you go back to (19) through the hole in the theater wall, you'll take fire damage. It proves, once again, that you pay for convenience.

21 Use the red key to open the door, drop the Pig Cop and go up. When you step off the ramp the far wall explodes—more Pig Cops. Make some bacon, leap through the hole, and open the door at the end of the passage.

22 Take out the Pig Cops from the doorway. You can see the Nuke badge that ends the level across the bridge. Not so fast, Dukie. Instead, leap onto the ledge to your lower right, just as you step onto the bridge. It's a narrow ledge, but walkable.

23 Secret place. Follow the ledge around the building (picking up a medkit) to the palm tree. Save the game, then jump onto the treetop. Face the building and leap through a window, either a little to the left or right (the wall is solid directly in front of you). Grab the goodies and go back to (22). If you defoliated the tree, you'll need to use the jet pack to gain access.

24 Secret place. Get out the RPG and fire up the jet pack. Face the wall with the ground-level exit, angle your aim up and to the right, and fly to the top. Take out the turrets and duck into the alcove. You should be almost out of jet pack fuel, but the designers thoughtfully put another pack in the alcove for you. Jet down safely and say good-bye to Tinseltown (25).

MISSION 2:
RED LIGHT DISTRICT

We suspect some people will take issue with this mission. In our opinion, the hooker and dancing girls add a certain, uh, lusty flair and bit-mapped appeal to L.A.'s fetid underside. There's no doubt these female characters make juicy targets, and killing them can be justified by the fact they're really Aliens in female bodies—a topic we neither have the room nor desire to address. If only those Aliens would stop stealing our chicks!

We should note that when you complete the mission, and let these chicks live to dance another day, you will get a "0" for the number of remaining enemies. In other words, you only get credit for the monsters you kill—the hooker and dancers don't affect your final score. But how you play it is, of course, up to you.

Warning: At the end of this level you'll be stripped of everything you've collected, except for your health, your cunning, and fighting skills. In other words, be liberal with your ammo, because you can't take it with you.

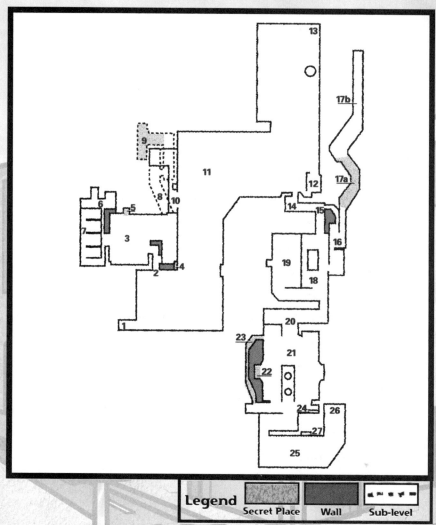

HIGHLIGHTS

- All eight secret places
- All six basic weapons
- All three basic varieties of monsters

Mission 2: Red Light District At-A-Glance

1 Start

2 Fire hydrant, pistol

3 Aliens, pistol ammo, monitor, shotgun

* 4 Healing Atom, Holoduke

* 5 Armor, pipebombs

6 Medkit, night vision goggles, toilet

7 Pistol ammo, medkit, steroids, RPG

8 Button lock (* * *)

* 9 Healing atom, pistol ammo

10 RPG ammo, medkit (in trash can), chaingun & ammo, blue key card, switch

11 Medkits, pistol ammo, armor

12 Blue key lock, button lock (* * * *), demolition switch

13 RPG ammo, yellow key, portable medkit, manhole

14 Yellow key lock, shotgun, medkit

15 Vent to 16

16a & 16b Toilets, medkit, secret door to 17a & 17b; shotgun ammo (in trashcan)

* 17a & 17b RPG ammo, Holoduke, steroids, medkit, night vision goggles; pipebombs, Healing Atom. (Can be accessed from the manhole at 13)

18 Pistol ammo (in trash can)

19 Monitor, red key, chaingun ammo, pistol & ammo, Pig Cop raid, O.J. joke

20 Pig Cop raid, red key lock

21 Shotgun ammo, medkit, trigger for (22)

* 22 Chaingun & ammo

* 23 Healing Atom, pipebombs, monitor, pistol ammo

* 24 Curtain switch, medkit, night vision goggles

25 Nothing but enemies

26 End

* 27 Portable medkit

* Denotes secret place

Duke-Anne,
You'd Better Shoot Out the Red Light

1 Start. Watch for flying Pig Cops and Aliens when you leap out. Dash left. The bookstore awning provides excellent cover.

2 Heal up with the fire hydrant water, if necessary, and enter the bookstore through the left side of the door. A Pig Cop doorman awaits his destiny.

3 Stir up the Aliens. Use the bookshelves and corners to your advantage! Dash around the counter and go all the way to the monitor. Leap up onto the bookcase opposite the monitor to get a Healing Atom. From there, face the corner and hit the [Spacebar] to open (4).

4 Secret place. Holy Duke Nukem! Come to poppa!

5 Secret place. Hit the [Spacebar] in front of the third-from-the-left bookcase. It swings wide open. Take your prizes, you've earned them.

6 Take a right down the hall and go into the bathroom. Watch for Aliens! Hit the hand-drying machine to reveal a alcove containing night vision goggles. Leave the john and go down to the other end of the hall. Use the Holoduke at the intersection to draw out a waiting Pig Cop.

7 Besides Pig Cops and Aliens, here's what you'll find in the peep show stalls, down the line:

   1 Pistol ammo in the trashcan
   2 Medkit
   3 Steroids in the trashcan
   4 RPG behind the viewscreen door.

   Note puckered wall next to curtain D. Blow the wall to gain access back to (6).

8 Open the door lock by pressing the outer-two buttons. When it's unlocked, it will look like this: * * *. Before you go in, launch a rocket down the hallway and flip on your night goggles.

9 Secret place. Turn right just before the elevator. Watch for lurking aliens! Go to the "T" intersection, turn left.When you cross into the lighted area the "Secret Place" message appears. Battle the Pig Cop for the Healing Atom. Work your way back to the elevator. Face right and ride up.

10 The blue key is behind the small red panel. Dash through the second room for the chaingun ammo. Aliens in the street will break the window (if you haven't already) and start shooting. Even so, this book depository window makes a great place to snipe at flying vehicles with your chaingun. The switch to the left of the window reveals a cool Duke joke. It also generates more monsters. You can leap out of the window to riot in the street—position (11)—and take damage in the fall, or go back through the bookstore. A Pig Cop waits for you in (8) if you backtrack.

11 Climb up the outcropping that's next to the burning trash-can. Go left and follow the ledge around the corner grab some armor. Drop down and go into the demolition chamber (12).

12 Insert the blue key. Activate the middle two buttons (* * * *), then hit the switch. Holy cow!

13 Jump over the far-left corner of the rubble. You'll find: a box of RPG rockets to your left; a yellow key at the top right; and a portable medkit and manhole cover at the bottom right. Dispose of the Pig Cop and blow the manhole cover with an explosive, if you want. It leads to (17b), which from this way leads to (17a) and then dead ends. Instead, let's use the yellow key to go into the bar and brawl.

14 Use the yellow key to get in. Hammer the reception committee and grab the goodies. Shoot out the grate up the nearby ramp.

15 Worm through the vent.

16a & 16b From the safety of the vent, toss a pipebomb into the men's room to clean it out. Take out the monsters in (16b) to prevent a sneak attack while you lap up the healing toilet water. Go to the only commode stall in (16a), nestle up against the back wall, and press the [Spacebar].

17a Secret place. Draw the Pig Cops through this funnel of death. Go down the ramp, grab the goodies and run back. You've just triggered your first Octabrain into action. Like the Pig Cops, let it come to you.

17b Secret place. Jump across the flowing waste for a box of pipebombs. Hug the walls and go down the sewer to claim a Healing Atom. Do what you will with the cocoon.

18 Take out the Aliens, then play a game of pool if you like— and if you think all this killing is making Duke thirsty, you're in luck. A nearby watering hole beckons.

19 Battle your way into the bar. Clean out the riffraff, but don't go behind the bar yet! Drop a few pipebombs at the bar's entrance and then ease backward behind the bar. You've just triggered a Pig Cop raid. Hit the trigger and...oooooh, ahhhh. Duck behind the door to the bottom right of the register to snatch the red key. Face the hooker and the TV set. If you read the mission introduction, you know what your choices are. Follow the signs to the dance club.

> **Note!**
>
> The TV screen depicts the most infamous chase scene ever—O.J.'s low-speed white Bronco "chase" down the freeways of L.A.

20 It's an uphill battle against a horde of Pig Cops. Toss a few pipebombs over the crest the ramp, but not too far!. When you crest the ramp, the far ceiling blows open. Another Pig Cop ambush! Lur them towards the pipebombs you so lovingly laid. Once the smoke clears, unlock the door and get ready to boogie.

21 Break up the party. The shotgun ammo is around the left of the garage door. The medkit is in the far left corner. Stand on the row of seats near to the shotgun ammo to open (22). You'll have to haul-ass to get there before the door closes. Do what you will with the dancers. Killing the center dancer triggers a pair of Aliens behind her. The deaths of the other four dancers trigger a total of three Aliens. Once the room is cleared to your satisfaction, shoot out the grate near the left corner and jump in to (23).

22 Secret place. Chaingun & ammo.

23 Secret place. Shoot out the far grate and toss a few pipebombs through the hole. Jump down to the backstage area and battle to the far end of the stage. Note that you can get backstage by pressing a button along the lip of the stage, on the right-hand side.

24 Secret place. The switch opens the curtains and reveals more baddies. The secret place is on a ledge above the switch. You can leap to this area from the lip of the backstage loft. Here's how:

☞ open the curtain and bounce the baddies out;

☞ jump on the dais where the Pig Cop stood (between the center dancer and the backstage loft); and,

☞ jump to the loft.

25 Clear this area with RPG fire. There is an abundance of Pig Cops.

26 Perform a long distance disposal of the guard in this alcove, but don't enter it yet! Backtrack to (27).

27 Secret place. Press the lighted wall between the crates. Go in for a portable medkit. After boosting your health, head back towards (26) and succumb to the mission-ending trap. As the trap is sprung, you can use up any remaining RPGs on the Pig Cops that taunt you. End.

Tip!

Max out your health points before you cross into the alcove marked (26)! You're about to walk into a trap set by those Alien bastards. You've always wanted to visit Death Row, haven't you?

MISSION 3: DEATH ROW

You begin with a ride on Old Sparky—with the smell of your own burning flesh fouling your nose. It's time for a jail break (with a little AC/DC in the background)—take no prisoners. In order to make your escape, you have to do a fair amount of tedious backtracking. No one said jail was all fun and games. This mission also introduces you to your first underwater experience. Why? You have to gain access to a nuclear sub. Unfortunately, the sub will sink with you in it! Man. Only a hero of Duke Nukem's caliber could possibly survive....

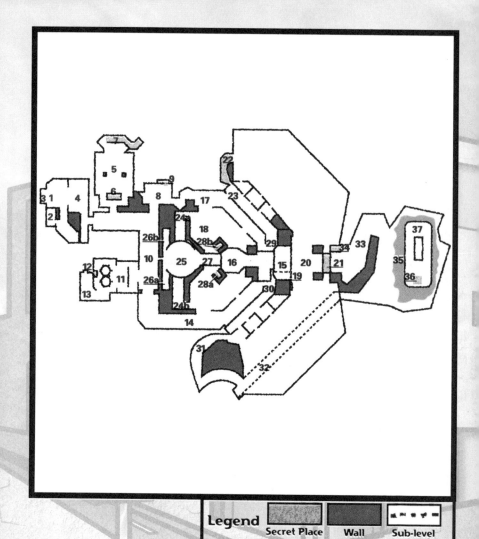

Legend
Secret Place   Wall   Sub-level

HIGHLIGHTS

- All 10 secret places
- Certified scuba time

MISSION 3: DEATH ROW AT-A-GLANCE

1 Start, medkits

2 Pistol & ammo, medkit, switches

3 Shotgun & ammo

4 Holoduke, portable medkit

5 Pistol ammo, medkits, steroids

* 6 Armor, Healing Atoms

* 7 Chaingun

8 Medkit, cocoon, toilet, pistol ammo

* 9 RPG ammo

10 Medkit

11 Chaingun ammo

*12 Healing Atom, night vision goggles

13 Shotgun ammo, medkit, RPG, monitor, blue key card

14 Blue key lock

15 Boots, medkits, pistol ammo

16 Yellow key card, shotgun ammo, monitor

17 Canisters, Healing Atom (tunnel back to 8)

18 Medkits, yellow key lock, shotgun ammo, pistol, monitor

19 RPG ammo, medkit, monitor

20 Lower deck: medkits, pistol ammo, shotgun ammo, red key Upper deck: pistol ammo, pipebombs, chaingun ammo

*21 Healing Atoms

*22 Steroids

23 Chaingun ammo, canister

24a & 24b Red key lock, pistol ammo; red key lock, medkit

25 Chaingun, medkit, armor (in vent shaft)

26a & 26b Switch for cell block 01, monitor, pistol ammo; switch for cell block 02, monitor, pipebomb

27 Map

*28a & 28b Healing Atom; pipebombs

29 Pistol ammo, shotgun ammo, RPG, medkit

30 Shotgun ammo, medkit, girlie poster, pistol ammo

31 Pipebombs

32 Shotgun ammo, medkit

33 Shotgun ammo, medkit, scuba gear, switch to open locked door in (20)

*34 Night vision goggles

35 Pistol ammo

*36 Portable medkit

37 Shotgun ammo, switch & periscope monitor, End

*Denotes secret place

DEAD DUKE WALKING

1   Start. Jump out of the chair! Hold the ⬆ while the mission loads—this ejects you out of the electric chair before you can take damage. Medkits are to your left.

2   A pistol and ammo are behind the panel just to the left as you enter this room, and you need to load up in a hurry. Drop the Pig Cop—quickly! The switch to the left of the window opens (3). The switch to the right opens (4). Open (3) only for now.

3   Jump down behind the chair, grab the shotgun and ammo. Go back to (2) and hit the other switch to open (4).

4   After you unload your shells into the peanut gallery, grab the Holoduke awaiting you behind the discolored wall panel on the right (as you face the hallway). I'll bet you need the portable medkit that's at the end of the hall. Be aware of a Pig Cop waiting to ambush you from the doorway on the left.

5   In an open space like the chapel, draw the Aliens to you. Shoot out the stained glass windows. The right conceals 'roids; the left leads to secret place (7).

6   Secret place. Stand against the middle of the far wall and shoot the switch above the pulpit—turning on the crosshairs makes hitting this button a lot easier. You'll ride a platform up to a secret nook. Shoot the hanging monk and grab the Healing Atom his spattered body coughs up.

7   Secret place. Press the image in front of the pulpit that resembles the Shroud of Turin. You'll know right away when you hit it. Yeesh. All that stands between you and a chaingun is a lone Octabrain. Go through the passage to the left of the cross and claim your prize. You have to jump over the dead space marine (and into the hellfire) to get it, or dispose of the body with weapons fire.

8   The barred door is unlocked. Duck into the hole in the right wall for pistol ammo. Stand next to the bench and hit the Spacebar. It swings out to reveal secret passage (9) with RPG ammo. Now, if only you actually had an RPG. . . .

9   Secret place. RPG ammo only.

10 When you cross the second band of light, the wall to your right explodes. A batch of Aliens bum rush you. Bastards. In case you need it, the medkit is on your left, just before the ramp.

11 Go in and clean out the Aliens, and save your game. If you're playing in God Mode, turn it off before you leap onto the gears. If you're divinely protected and you miss the jump and fall in, you may not get crushed, but you'll hang up your computer (even the hand of "God" has limits). Now *that* sucks.

    Leap onto the shorter gear then leap to the ledge with the Healing Atom. Follow the ledge all the way around to the left and hit the [Spacebar] for a set of night vision goggles.

12 Secret place. A Healing Atom and night vision goggles are yours—if you don't fall and get squished. Leapfrog to the higher gear to the clear, well-lighted place (13).

13 Ahhhh, a gaggle of wimpy Aliens and the blessed RPG. The blue key is behind the far panel. You only have to jump down onto the first gear to escape.

14 Use the blue key to unlock the door. Next, you have a choice: you can go through the door to your left (marked Control East), or duck under the electric eye and go up the ramp— I recommend the later. If Old Sparky didn't fry your ass, these will. Big time. Take out the Pig Cops in (18) from the window sill on the ramp. The coppers are easy prey from this height.

    The top of the ramp leads to cell blocks 01 & 02 (29 and 30 respectively), (16), the yellow key card room; and (15), the shower room. Don't worry about the Pig Cops behind the forcefields. Even though you can open any one of the cells with the appropriate switch, the Aliens inside won't come out of their cells to battle the Pig Cops for you. Even so, I suggest that you open the third cell door in cell block 01—it contains an RPG and medkit you can get at (23).

15 Enter the shower room through either door (they're framed by yellow and black stripes). The boots are in the middle stall. Now, let's get the yellow key!

16 The yellow key looks booby trapped, right? In fact, as soon as you pick up the yellow key, a trio of high electric eyes snap on and Pig Cops come sniffing around. Slide sideways and the Pig Cops will step into the beams you jumped over. Cool. Don't let them get too close or their stupidity will rip you to shreds, too.

17 Take out the Pig Cop and blow the canisters from a distance. Go in the hole for a Healing Atom. You've completed a tunnel to (8). If you put on your night vision goggles you'll see the message "Behind the Babe"—which you couldn't see when you first got into (8) because you didn't have the goggles. That message is very important, for it's a hint on how to get out of this mission!

18 Go through the door marked Control West. The yellow key lock is to your left, down the ramp.

19 A single well-placed RPG shot into the right alcove makes mincemeat out of the waiting piggys. Grab the goodies, read text for (20), take a deep breath, then go through the next door.

20 Like other similar huge areas, I won't force you do it my way. Even so, here are the tactics that worked for me. They should work for you, too:

☞ Take out all four turrets with your RPG. The turrets are positioned to make sure you're always caught in a nasty crossfire. Though you might take some heavy damage, you'll be glad you did this now. A word of advice: don't stand around slack-jawed and watch your shot hit! Use your brains and your ears instead. Using the doorways for cover, jump out, aim, fire, leap back, and listen. Just so you know, the door across from where you entered is locked—and the switch to open it is on its other side.

☞ Hug the cell block wall and go all the way around to the left for the red key.

☞ Launch an RPG shot at the puckered wall above the red key—that's secret place (22).

☞ Return the fire of the enemies on the windows above. These are the individual cells in cell blocks 01 & 02. It's hard for Aliens to snipe at you from their cells at this oblique angle. The second cell from the left has a weak spot in the wall. If you launch an RPG shot in to it, a hole opens, which lets a few Aliens escape—that is if you don't lob an RPG round in the hole. Heh, heh.

- Crawl up either outcropping that flanks the locked door across from where you came in. Leap up to the turret deck area. Scour the area for pistol ammo, chaingun ammo, and pipebombs, but watch out! On this death tier, the Aliens in the windows have a much better shot at you.

- On the upper deck, climb up either side of the tower. The wall looks solid, but it isn't. This is secret place (21).

- Go to the hole above where the red key was located. If you ran out of RPG rounds, detonate a pipebomb below it on the upper deck. Leap in to secret place (22).

21 Secret place. Yes! Healing Atoms.

22 Secret place. Toss a pipebomb against the puckered wall and get your favorite weapon to the ready. You're about to enter the cell block 01 through the back door. Take the RPG and medkit from the cell you opened at (14).

23 Shoot the canister. It blows open a hole that looks into (17). That's good, because we have the red key and we're going to backtrack to (18).

24a & 24b The red key opens both doors. The only difference is that (24a) gives you a pistol clip and (24b) has a medkit (each usually guarded by a Pig Cop). Either ramp takes you to a switch that opens room (25).

25 The chaingun in the Alien holohead isn't boobytrapped. The vent shaft contains some armor. Go for it, dude. Hit either switch next to either door and step back—you'll be squished if you just stand there. The left hall leads to room (26a); the right to (26b).

> **Note!**
>
> The vent shaft leads back to (10). If you finish the mission and still
> have two monsters left to kill, know that they materialized when you
> went through the door at (14). If you want a 100 percent kill rating,
> here's a way to sneak up on them from behind. You will take damage
> from the fall, however.

26a Hit the switch so that the red light is on. The forcefield to cell
     block 01 is now deactivated. You've done well, Obi wan.

26b Repeat your actions from (26a) here. If you ran out of
     pipebombs before you got here, you get one here—and
     you'll need it to get into (27).

27 In (25) hit the switch to make the room spin. You should see
    a large red door. Open it, jump back, and toss a pipebomb
    into the electric eyes. Blammo! Go down the catwalk, stand
    against the wall and hit [Spacebar]—oh boy, a map of this
    mission! Two alcoves also opened—one to your upper right
    (28a) and one to our upper left (28b).

28a & 28b Secret places. Get yer Healing Atom and a side-order
    of pipebombs to go! Very yin-yang. Now it's time to investi-
    gate the individual cells.

29 Cell block 01. Each time you depress the "knife" switch
    you open a cell door. You can only open one at a time, so
    this means opening a door, cleaning out the cell, running
    back to the switch to open the next cell, etc. It's a labori-
    ous process, but there it is. Here are the items in each cell
    of this block, down the row, starting at the cell closest to
    the switch:

       1 Pistol ammo
       2 Shotgun ammo, pistol ammo
       3 RPG, medkit

    Look out the windows. See the turret towers? You've dug
    your own grave if you didn't already take them out.

30 Cell block 02. Down the row you'll find:

> 1 Shotgun ammo
> 2 Medkit
> 3 Pistol ammo, girlie poster
> 4 Pistol ammo (at the end of the hallway)

   Walk into the girlie poster—it conceals a tunnel. Hmmmmm. Those gol-durn Aliens were digging their way out, a-la *Shawshank Redemption*. Better investigate.

31 Pipebomb the puckered wall. Lob a pipebomb (or launch an RPG shot) through the flames to break open yet another weak wall. Doing so means you only have to go through the raging fire once. If you're out of explosives, you'll have to dash through the fire to get the pipebombs in front of the second weak spot, and then go back though fire to stand clear of the blast. Ummmm, toasty.

32 Jump over the sludge, hug a wall, get out your RPG, and go with the flow. You should be able to see the sub and monsters just before you round the bend. It'll take them a few seconds to see you—just enough time to blow them to smithereens. The beach area is a good place to drop a Holoduke if you're unable to smear the Octabrains and Aliens from the sewage pipe.
   Duke's line upon sighting the sub is a good clue of where we're going...but not just yet.

33 Watch for a Pig Cop ambush! This is the backside of the locked door in (20). Hmmmmm, I wonder what that scuba gear is for?

34 Secret place. Leap onto the tower's right outcropping , face the steel wall, and hit the [Spacebar]. Duck in for your newest pair of night vision goggles.

35 Soften up the water with a few pipebombs then dive in. Unless you want the pistol ammo, don't bother exploring this waterworld—you need to reserve as much oxygen as possible for the next mission. Take Duke Cousteau under the sub and go up through the hole in the bottom of the vessel. Watch for Aliens when you pop up!

36 Secret place. Go to the back wall of the sub, right-side of center. Press the [Spacebar] and go into the secret room. You can't destroy the engine, but you can grab the nearby portable medkit. I shouldn't have to say this, but don't try to crawl into the reaction chamber, the forcefield gives you quite a shock—after all, you're on a metal deck and your feet are wet....

37 End. You'd best grab a snorkel 'cause we're going down! Go to the front of the sub. Hit the nuke badge to complete this sub mission.

MISSION 4: TOXIC DUMP

This is by far our favorite mission in Episode One. You get to swim with the Octabrains; gulp steroids and leap across chasms; get small; duck into nuclear reaction chambers; ride toxic sluge rivers; and of course, deal out bloody bucket loads of death.

This level also has the classic ticking clock built right into your oxygen tank—the last thing you want to do is run out of air. In order to prevent this cruel death, a demise totally unbefitting a hero like Duke Nukem, we recommend you rely heavily on your RPG, pipebombs and Holoduke(s). Don't do anything fancy underwater—just bring Scooba-Duke into rocket-range and give 'em hell.

If you rely on quicksaves, you *can* complete every aspect of this mission by using only the items you find here—even on the highest difficulty setting. You don't need cheats, you just need this book....

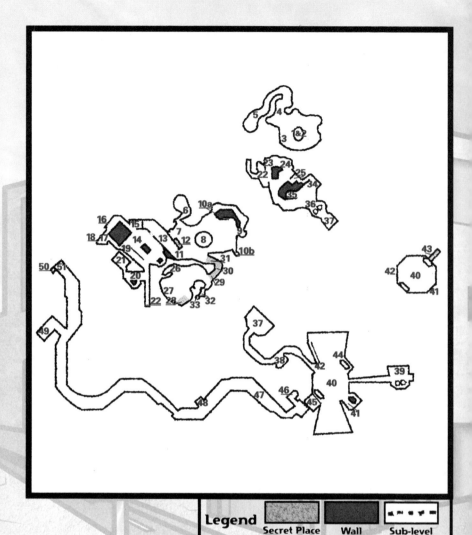

Legend

| Secret Place | Wall | Sub-level |

HIGHLIGHTS

- All 14 secret places
- Access to the secret Mission 6
- The shrink ray—so you can get small

MISSION 4: TOXIC DUMP AT-A-GLANCE

1 Start
2 Button puzzle (* * *)
3 Scuba gear
4 Pistol ammo, portable medkit, puckered wall
5 Healing Atom, pipebombs
* 6 Cocoon, puckered wall
7 Sub pen
8 Medkit, RPG, blue key
* 9 Armor, Healing Atom, portable medkit
*10a RPG ammo
10b Cryptic message
11 Blue key door
*12 Chaingun
13 Chaingun ammo
14 Shotgun ammo
15 Shotgun, monitor, medkit, red key
*16 Chaingun ammo
17 Armor, monitor, Healing Atom
*18 Healing Atoms
19 Chaingun ammo, scuba gear, cocoon
20 Red key lock (for shrink ray), monitor
21 Lock for door at (20), medkit
22 Medkits, shotgun ammo
23 Mines, night vision goggles, locked door into (34)
24 Chaingun & ammo
25 Shotgun ammo, switch to raise water level
26 Chaingun ammo, steroids

27 Medkits
*28 RPG ammo, portable medkit, shotgun
*29 Puckered wall
*30 Healing Atom
*31 Shortcut back into (7)
32 RPG, medkit, switch to open door 02 at (23)
*33 Shotgun ammo, scuba gear
34 Shotgun ammo, switches
35 Chaingun ammo
36 Gears, portable medkit
37 Shotgun ammo
*38 Medkit, teleport to 39
*39 RPG ammo
40 Shotgun ammo, medkit
41 Pipebombs, chaingun ammo, medkit, monitor, switch to open (42)
42 Button
*43 RPG & ammo
44 Shotgun ammo
45 Healing Atom, chaingun ammo
*46 Healing Atoms
47 Medkits, chaingun ammo
48 RPG ammo, boots
*49 Chaingun ammo, End—access to secret mission (Launch Facility)
50 Teleport to areas (26-33)
51 End

* Denotes secret place

I'VE GOT A SUB-MARINE MISSION FOR YOU, BABY

1   Start.

2   Sink beneath the rising water to the button lock. Like the other three-button lock in Mission 2, the combination is; * * *. Go through the emergency hatch (it's on your upper right), RPG to the ready.

3   Punish the local Octabrains and grab the scuba gear in the sea weeds. Instead of surfacing, go into the cave.

4   Blow out the puckered wall (and if you're lucky, you can nuke the Octabrain with the same shot).

5   Swim up the passage into the room, drop a Holoduke at the entrance, swim backward and blast those bad brains. Collect the goods and *up periscope.*

6   Secret place. The lip of ground is actually the secret place. Don't worry, the barrels don't explode, *DOOM*-style. Just get your RPG ready and blast through the wall. You're in for a fight.

7   Take out the Aliens in the pillbox. Look to your left—that's the *USS Dallas.* Use the pillar for cover while you take out the turrets and the Aliens in (8).

8   You'll be caught in a turret cross fire the moment you grab the blue key. Those Aliens are so crafty. The turrets are in tiny alcoves to your right and left. Creep out and lob an RPG shot into each one **before** you grab the key. You should be able to leap to the right one—which is (10a)—no problem. You need a gulp of 'roids and a jet pack to make it into (10b).

9   Secret place. Run through the fire on top of the *Dallas.* You've opened a secret panel inside the sub. Go back into the sub and go all the way to the top to collect your swag.

> **Tip!**
>
> If you have trouble making the jumps, try hitting
> [F7] and using the Chase View to get the perspec-
> tive you need. We found this to be the easiest way
> to stick my landings.

10a Secret place. Hit the [Spacebar] next to the left wall, all the
   way back. A panel slides up to reveal RPG ammo.

10b The far left wall opens to reveal a secret message. So, how did
   you get there?

11 Get your shotgun out and use the blue key and go on in to
   Long Beach's newest nuclear waste facility.

12 Secret place. The wall slides open on the right side of the
   cooridor, just past the bend. The secret place is just as you
   enter. However, turn right and hit the [Spacebar] and enter
   the pillbox where the caged Aliens were. Exit the same way
   you came in.

13 Another Alien awaits around the next bend, next to the red
   door. If you time your attack right, you can shotgun the
   Alien into the electric eyes. Not only is it a cool effect, it lib-
   erates the chaingun ammo. The silver door is locked (but
   you can open it from (15)).

14 There are myriad ways through this room. I'll take you the
   most linear way through:

   ☞ Jump down to the main floor.

   ☞ Let the claw pick up at least one barrel.

   ☞ Stand on the striped platform and let the claw pick you
     up.

   ☞ On the next conveyer belt you'll fight an Alien. Make
     sure a barrel gets picked up before you do. In other
     words, shoot the Alien but not the barrel. While in the

air, this barrel will trip an electric eye (that was meant for you if you went through too fast).

☞ Let the claw grab you and haul you to (15).

15 Immediately shoot out the glass to your right and take out the Pig Cop. The red key is behind the red door. You can also unlock the silver door at (13) from here. Step back onto the conveyer belt.

16 Secret place. Jump off the conveyer belt into the lava slime and open the left-most wall for chaingun ammo. Keep on riding.

17 Shoot out the glass before you get to the room. Entering the room triggers a few Aliens to attack from the conveyer belt. Take them out, then hit the blue switch on the far wall to open the reactor chambers. Against your better judgement, crawl into the left most chamber and jump—the ledge you land on is secret place (18). Take the Healing Atom from the right reactor while you're at it.

18 Secret place. What more logical place could you find Healing Atoms but on a ledge in a nuclear reactor? Jump in and up. Yum.

19 Go against the conveyer belt's direction to get to (19). If you stay on it, you'll get dumped onto the striped platform where you started this assembly line gig.

   You can't just go to (19)—you have to trigger an ambush! When you cross into the lighted area (20), a horde of Pig Cops will come out from the right. Once you've ground them into pork bellies, go up the ramp for the scuba gear.

20 The red door here is locked. The red key lock is on the far wall. If only it were that easy. . . . This is a wall-mounted shrink ray. Activate the ray, get small, and go through the right-side vent. Keep going to your right and you'll come into (21).

   FYI: The left vent empties out where the Pig Cops ambushed you at (19); and if you take a left at the "T" intersection when in the right vent, you are routed back into (20).

21 Get big, smush the Aliens, hit the lock to open the red door at (20), get small, and go back the way you came. Close the

door at (20) after you've gone through to avoid any more shrinkage. Plunge into the drink, RPG to the ready.

22 Welcome to waterworld. It's a safe room from which to sweep out the mines to your right. Loop around to the right or left to stir up the Octabrains.

23 Watch out for any missed mines as you swim around the center column enroute to (25). Along the way you'll stir up a batch of Octabrains. A shotgun blast takes out the mines quite nicely—especially if an Octabrain is nearby. The door marked "02" is locked. Hmmmmmm.

24 When the far mine on the left is detonated, a wall blows open to reveal a chaingun and ammo. Don't let the Octabrains pin you into a corner. Remember, you're swimming in a three-dimensional environment—up and down is as good as left and right.

25 Hit the switch on the lower right and watch the water level rise. Yowza. Get yer weapon of choice ready and go forward and up. You can't open the silver door from here (but you can from the other side, at (33)).

26 Jump on the ledge for the ammo and 'roids. In a few moments you'll need the latter to reach secret place (28).

27 Gulp yer 'roids and jump off the smaller lip on the right into the large, square hole in the wall. (Note: Look at the figure on the next page for a shortcut!)

28 Secret place. Switch on your night vision goggles. The secret place is actually the ledge that holds the portable medkit (you have to jump onto the ledge to activate the message). Go back to (27) and leap off the left lip.

29 Secret place. Blow the puckered wall, take out the Alien and go in. Another puckered wall?

30 Secret place. Grab the Healing Atom and blow away the already weak wall.

31 Secret place. You've carved yourself a shortcut back into the sub pen (7).

Figure 4-1. The X marks the spot! Behind the crosshairs is a false wall that hides a teleport to (50). Talk about a shortcut! If you 'roid up you may be able to jump in. If not, cheat a little, give yourself the jet pack, and you can literally fly to the finish. To get back to (27), you have to jet pack against the raging sludge flow to activate the teleport.

32 Hit the switch beneath the "02" (you can raise and lower the water level with the switch on the orange cylinder—at this point it doesn't matter what the water level is). Now put 02 and 02 together and. . . but first, a secret place.

33 Secret place. Open the wall between the monitor and the orange cylinder. Ahhh, life-giving air and life-saving shotgun ammos. Time for more water sports.

34 Swim like a madman through the now-opened door 02 and drop a Holoduke near the large doors to the right. Watch for an Octabrain ambush from below! A single RPG shot can take out all of Holoduke's friends. Once you've brained the Octo-groupies, go into the small room beyond the doors—this is room (34). You should:

    ☞ get out your shotgun and unlock the door;

    ☞ go into the hallway to get another Holoduke and battle another Octabrain—the hallway leads to (25);

    ☞ hit the switch next to the window (doing so opens the large steel doors); and,

☞ launch an RPG shot into room (35) to chunkify the Octabrain.

35 Go in for your swag.

36 The switch on the left closes the doors. Don't bother with it unless lots of Octabrains are still lurking about. Yes, you're going through the gears (be ready to dispose of Octabrains on the other side). Here's how:

☞ save your game;

☞ turn off God Mode, if you're in it;

☞ wait for the bluish stripes (missing gears) to converge and float in (the current will carry you through); and,

☞ get the portable medkit by riding around the gear where the tooth is missing.

37 Hop out of the water, blast the Aliens and claim the shotgun ammo. Then get out your RPG and float downstream.

38 Secret place. Use your ⬇ to keep from being swept past the puckered wall on the right, just before the passage curves to the right. This is also where the current picks up. Once you've opened the hole with an RPG shot, hug the right wall and you should pop in. This is very difficult to do, so a jet pack will come in very handy as you practice.
Get out your shotgun and leap into the teleporter.

39 Secret place. Only a few Aliens stand between you and two heaping boxes of RPG ammo. You can jump into the stream here or teleport back to (38)—it doesn't matter, because both lead into (40).

40 Unless you have the Ⓐ key jammed down, you'll go beneath the surface. That's good because you want to take out the Octabrains. Thank God there was a Holoduke back in (34). Surface and swim to the red platform.

41 Fight your way up to the switch. It opens area (42).

42 Slog up the waterfall, jump into the left door, and pick up the medkit.

43 This secret place is by far the most difficult area to access in the first episode. Here's how without cheating:

- ☞ get into the water next the moving platform at (44)—the platform should be between you and the red button at 42);

- ☞ shoot the red button and quickly drop beneath the waves;

- ☞ shoot out the fan hidden behind the moving platform; and,

- ☞ **turn off God Mode and save your game**—you can either:

    1 Stand on the center of the ledge—in (44)—just next to the niche in the platform, shoot the red button, and step off the ledge with the Z button depressed. You'll fall even with hole.

    2 Stay in the water, shoot the button, and swim inside.

The platform will woosh you into the alcove (or, alternately, squish you against the wall). Go up through the grating (above the ammo) to complete this area. The switch inside will move the platform so you can get out.

44 Slog up the water fall again, jump onto the right ledge. Stand on the moving platform, shoot the red button at (42), and step onto the other platform. Go to (45). Fun.

45 Shoot out the fan on the other side of the slime, then creep onto the ledge. Just as you're sucked off the ledge, leap into the hole where the fan was.

46 Secret place. Grab the Healing Atoms and get out.

47 Ride the slime river until the ledges appear. Rely on Holoduke to lure away the Octabrains. Once past (48) and the slime waves, the toxic river starts to haul. The ledges also disappear but the Octabrains keep coming.

48 Grab the boots and ammo and keep going.

49 Secret place and end. Hug the left wall as the current sweeps you down. Yeeeehaaa!!! Use your ↓ to slow you down. Just before the last left bend, you can see a puckered wall. RPG it

open. If you're close enough to the left wall you should hang up an a small ledge. (If you miss the ledge, you won't be able to run against the current—even if you're on 'roids—but you can backtrack against the current by jumping or using your jet pack. You have to cheat and jet pack back.) Waste the Aliens and go to the Launch Facility. Or, go back into the slime and end at (51) if you have something against secret missions. Note: successfully completing the secret mission takes you to Mission 5.

50 Go through the red door if you want. The teleport takes you to areas (26-33).

51 End.

MISSION 5: ABYSS

Now that you've crawled out of the water, it's time to fly. It's evolution, Duke'm style. Even though this is labeled Mission 5, you battle the Alien boss and finish this episode. (Mission 6 is the secret mission you access in room (49) of the Mission 4 walk-through). At the very least, to defeat the final boss you should have:

➤ the jet pack from secret Mission 6—it's in room (17) of that mission's walk-through;

➤ 50 RPG rockets;

➤ 200 health points; and,

➤ this walk-through.

If you follow my path through the mission and save often, you won't use a drop of jet pack juice until you encounter the big boss himself—which is where you're going to need every ounce of it. Now, get ready to rumble!

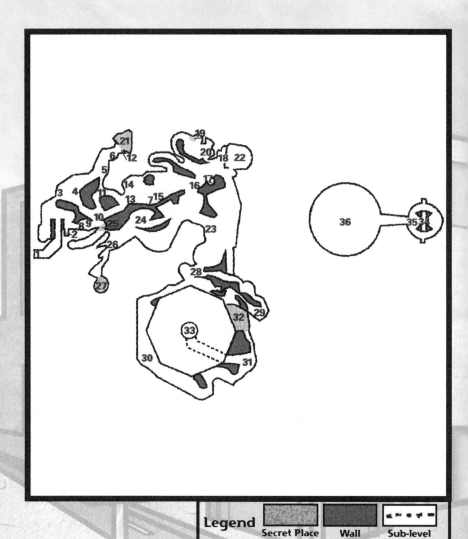

HIGHLIGHTS

- All six hidden secrets
- Battle the baddest Alien boss so far
- Springboard into Episode Two

Mission 5: Abyss At-a-Glance

1 Start, medkits

2 Shotgun ammo, boots

3 Shotgun, medkit, pistol ammo

4 Chaingun ammo, shotgun ammo, medkits, pistol ammo, pistol

5 Chaingun ammo, medkit, chaingun

6 Cactus, blue key, medkit, shotgun ammo

7 Medkits, night vision goggles

8 RPG, blue key lock

9 Medkits, pipebombs, cryptic message

10 RPG ammo

11 Chaingun ammo, bridge, medkit

12 Night vision goggles, chaingun ammo, portable medkit

13 Cacti, historical site marker, Healing Atoms

14 Holoduke, boots, portable medkit

15 Medkits, cacti

16 Shotgun

17 Medkit, hand switch, portable medkit

18 Healing pool, chaingun, boots, medkit

*19 Steroids

20 Pipebombs, RPG, night vision goggles

21 RPG ammo, Healing Atoms

**22 Medkits, hand switches, shrink ray, trigger for area (28)

23 Shotgun ammo

24 Medkits, chaingun ammo, shotgun ammo, boots, pipebombs.

*25 Shotgun ammo, medkit, pistol ammo, chaingun ammo

26 Hand switch

*27 Healing Atoms

28 Medkit, Healing Atoms

29 Boots, portable medkit, shotgun ammo, Healing Atom

30 Cryptic message, RPG & ammo

31 Chaingun ammo, armor

*32 Healing Atom

33 Medkit, chaingun ammo

34 RPG, chaingun & ammo

35 RPG ammo, chaingun ammo

36 End, portable medkit, RPG ammo, Healing Atom, cocoon women, chaingun ammo, armor, jet pack

*Denotes secret place

Don't Go with the Flow!

1   Start. Hug the right wall and battle your way down the ledge. What a view! Keep turning right and go to the door.

2   After you grab the boots and ammo, go back to the mouth of the sludge waterfall. Leap across to the opposite ledge. A turret will start taking pot shots at you when you step onto the left ledge. This is a good target to silence with a precious RPG round. Go down the ramp to the supplies and lurking Octabrains.

3   Dive into the sludge river and get as far to the left as you can. If you're far enough over, you should hang up on a ledge just as you go over the falls. If not, you're going to (14). It's an incredibly fast river and takes a lot of jet pack juice to get out.

4   I shouldn't have to say this, but be careful not to slip and fall into the slime river when you're battling Aliens! Scour the upper paths for goodies, then go down the rock ramp. If you do slip and fall, you end up at (14).

5   Just beyond the chaingun ammo is an alcove with a fire. Smoke the Octabrain and nab his chaingun. Go back up to (4) and go turn right (this is the left-most ledge you saw after you went over the falls).

6   Snake along the ledge (blow up the cactus—you'll take damage from the cactus if you get too close to it), and you'll see the blue key. You'll have to jump on its dais to get it. If you're harassed by Aliens on the ledge above, why not take out a pipebomb while you're on the dais, jump up, and heave. If you time it right, the pipebomb will land squarely at their feet. Nasty. Better get out an umbrella.

7   Return to (4) and leap over the slime river to the right ledge. Battle your way down to a small wall. Leap up into a clearing. A niche at the far end contains a pair of night vision goggles. Look up. On the ledge above, you can see what looks like a stone marker (13), and above that, glinting Healing Atoms. Don't waste precious jet pack juice to score those atoms. There's a better, more heroic way. Return to (4) and jump up the slime falls, salmon-boy.

8 Wade to the left of the big falls, leap up onto the ledge and lo!—the blue key lock and an RPG. You can't kill the Pig Cop from this side of the grating, which drops as soon as you insert the key. Once the smoke clears, snap on your night vision goggles and go into the dark.

9 The pipebombs are in a small niche to the far left. We'll take the graffiti's advice soon enough. Return to the light and go left.

10 Kill the Pig Cop and leap across the ledge into the big hole on the wall. You don't need 'roids to make this jump—just the Run Mode. If you miss this jump, you'll find yourself down slime river at area (14). Again.

11 Turn left at the fork and tightrope across the rickety bridge. I found it best to put down all weapons to make sure I stayed on the rope. Gently tap the ↑ key and traverse the rope one step at a time. You've already pipebombed the Aliens at (12) from (6), so take your time.

12 You're looking in on secret place (21). You can't get there from here, but you can grab the goods outside. Go back to (11) and go down the right branch of the tunnel.

13 To get to the cacti, you'll have to make the jump of your life. It'll be easier if you down some 'roids, but if you're good you don't need it. No matter how you get there (unless via jet pack), you'll probably take some needling from those nasty cacti—unless you blow them away with an RPG shot.

   Go up to the historical site marker and, Holy. . . . Though you can't see it, the ledge from (4) that led to (7) has fallen. Instead of backtracking, look over the ledge to the left of the marker. See the sloping ledge and the Healing Atom? You might as well jump. If you finesse it, you won't take any damage. See the next, lower ledge? Jump and heal thyself! Now drop into the slime river.

14 Crawl out of the slime for the Holoduke, boots, and medkit. Wade across the slime and run down to the far end of the large open area.

15 This is where (7) was before you brought the walls a-tumblin' down. When you get to the medkits, you'll trigger an Octabrain into action (on the higher levels). Once you've

dispatched him, step off the edge next to the medkits. There are two ledges, and once you've jumped, you can't get back—unless you jet pack it.

16 Strap on you night vision goggles and leap across the river into the opening. Drop the cops and procede. The top of the stairs is area (16)—the backside of the castle-like wall you could see at the bottom of (15). Dispatch the Alien and lob a pipebomb or three through the window. Detonate. Go down the stairs to the left and duck into the room on the right. What the hell happened here?

17 Kneel down to press the hand switch. The fire alter slides open, revealing an Alien and a portable medkit. Turn right after you exit the room.

18 Leap into the waterfall. You get 30 health points back just for going into the water. Ahhhh. Complete the healing process by lapping up the fountain's holy elixir and snatching the chaingun. You'll find the boots opposite the healing pool (in an alcove on the left wall that opens as you go toward the red area). Get them and go back to (16). Hug the right wall and follow the passage up.

19 Secret place. Press the third stretch of wall to the right of the last fire alcove in the hallway (before you actually get to the fire pit). You have to go all the way in to get the "Secret Place" message.

20 Drop down the closest niche in the fire pit wall after you've coaxed the locals to their doom. You'll land on a Healing Atom! Once in the fire pit you should:

☞ press the yellow hand button on the left to open a compartment with an RPG (the button on the left side of the image with white and red circles);

☞ press the right yellow hand;

☞ jump onto the now-open door and leap onto the ledge above it for the night vision goggles; and,

☞ step into the fire to go to secret place (21).

21 Two secret places in one! This is the room you saw at (12). When you get the Healing Atoms, an Octabrain will most likely appear. Stair-step jump to the alcove for the RPG ammo—this ledge counts as a secret place. Go back to (20) via the fire.

22 Battle out of (20) down the hallway—stay clear of the fire in the alcoves. You'll take damage when you jump into (22), but the medkits below offset the damage. The purpose of this room is to open area (28)—the final path to the show-down with the Alien boss. Quickly:

☞ press the right hand switch;

☞ go up the stairs—the earthquake is area (28) opening up—and press the hand switch;

☞ haul ass to the platform that rises to your right (you'll have to be quick!);

☞ hit the hand switch and wait a moment;

☞ get small;

☞ scurry out the small hole in the wall (next where you dropped in) and you're back in (18).

23 Turn left and go out into a hellishly red area. Outside at last! Go right, down the stone ramp. Hurry through the lava, hugging the right wall around as you go to the ledge. Watch for swarming Octabrains! You can go to the left and into area (28) to finish the level, or be more adventurous and go right. What are you waiting for? Let's explore some more.

Tip!

If you want, give yourself the jet pack (if you don't have it) and fly into the alcove with the shrink ray cannon. You'll find a cryptic message inside that's almost worth the valuable jet pack time. You cheater. Be sure to avoid the shrink ray or you'll take a lava bath!

24 Haul yourself onto the lower ledge (next to the slime water-fall with the red steam). Mountaineer your way up to the ledges and leap over the waterfall. Keep going through the passage to the right. Watch for lurking Octabrains. The boots are to your right, in the open area, as you near the crest of the passage. The pipebombs are next to the puck-ered wall. Hmmmmm.

25 Secret place. Blast open the weakened wall and keep going up. The secret place is at the very top, just before you step out into area (10). Go back down to where you found the last box of pipebombs.

26 Leap to the island in the lava flow and hit the hand switch. A rock panel slides open above the lava falls to your left. So? . . . jump up and in.

27 Secret place. Leap into the opening on the left. Go down the passage for the Healing Atoms and a sight for sore eyes. Duke clearly likes what he sees. . . . Note: the "Secret Place" message doesn't flash on when you enter. You can either ride the lava flow down to (28) or go back the same way you climbed up to this area—it depends on how much life is left in your boots. You'll take damage after going over the last lava falls.

28 Watch out for Octabrains and Aliens (from above) as you battle your way up the passageway. There's a reason why you're stumbling across all these Healing Atoms.

29 You can see the Alien flag ship from the window. Grab the boots while you're there and go down the passage. The portable medkit is in the clearing and the shotgun ammo and Healing Atom are little farther down the passage.

30 Leap from platform to platform. If you slip and fall, guess what? You're dead. There's no room for error this close to the end. Save between each leap and watch for Aliens and Octabrains. If you do miss a jump and forgot to save, quick-ly hit the J key to turn on your jet pack (if you've got it). But try to save your jet pack for the last room!

> **Note!**
>
> At the bottom of the first ledge is the inscription "Dopefish lives," courtesy of the good folks at Apogee. Dopefish is mentioned in other Apogee games, such as *Wacky Wheels* and *Rise of the Triad*.

31 You'll find the chaingun ammo in this large room after you've climbed the steps. Don't open the door to the vault yet! Instead, press the wall to the right and back of the door.

32 Secret place. Go up the passage and claim the Healing Atom. The actual secret place is the open plateau. You can fly around the back of the ship if you want, but there's no back door entrance. Damn.

33 Loads of Octabrains wait to usher you in—draw them out individually or in pairs. If you time it right, you can squish a few with the door. When you grab the last box of chaingun ammo, the huge door will open. The switch next to the door (on the left, inside) opens and closes it. The switch to the right (inside the door) opens the worm hole. C'mon. Let's waste this alien trash.

> **Note!**
>
> The Alien hand switches resemble those from the movie *Total Recall*; and in our opinion, if you've gotten this far without cheating, you are badder than any Arnold character.

34 Welcome to an H.R. Geiger-inspired fantasy land, *Alien*-style. It's a choice between jetting or jumping down the hole. I say jet. Two alcoves will open near the bottom of the shaft if you traverse the perimeter. One contains an RPG, the other a chaingun and loads of ammo.

35 As you work your way around the circular room, grab all the ammo that pops out to greet you. You can open the large green door from here, but don't go in yet! Read (36) to see what you're up against. Once you've maxed out your chaingun and RPG ammo supply, save your game, open the light green door, and go on in.

36 End. The last boss is baaaad. It takes the equivalent of about 45 RPG shots to bag him, or 4500 hit points; although, he does seem to have a weak spot in his head that allows you to dispatch him for a mere 25 RPGs. How good's your aim? He'd be impossible to kill if you weren't Duke Nukem; and next to impossible to down if you fight this boss on his terms without gobs of jet pack fuel, which you should have been saving for this encounter.

There are two ground-level (and hidden) trip wires on the entrance side of that tantalizing portable medkit. The first trip line closes the door to the room—trapping you. Uh oh. Crossing the second, thicker trip line energizes the boss into action (he pops up out of the hole on the other side of the lava flow, where the floor crests). It's worth noting that neither of these trips work until you actually touch the ground—which means you're free to jet pack around the room to grab what you need or see the sights.

I've devised two ways to take this bad boy down: the "Duke-pure Method" (which is essentially a knock down, drag out method), and the "Duke-savvy Method" (which relies on finesse and calculated strikes). Here are the details:

Duke-pure Method

Save your game. Jump across the second line and hit your jet pack. On the way up, immediately take out the cocoon woman on the far left (from left to right, they conceal a jet pack, RPG ammo, and armor). Keep your distance, dip, duck and weave while you fire RPG round after round at him. Height, speed, and maneuverability are your only advantages! Pick up health, ammo, and jet pack juice as necessary (and don't forget the race car driver analogy). Some finer tips include:

☞ Aim for his head—it seems to be his only weak point.

☞ Don't forget to employ your old buddies, Holoduke and steroids!

☞ Take advantage of the fact that the boss stands still as he fires; also, he's wide open to attack when launching his grenades. Constant movement and strafing will allow you to exploit these weaknesses.

Duke-savvy Method

OK. So you didn't follow my advice and you used up all you precious jet pack juice. He's beaten you to a pulp over and over again. What to do? Simple. Fight him on *your* terms. Here's how:

- Set off the first trip wire and run back into (35) before the door closes. You don't need 'roids to make it, but you'll have to run. You've just outsmarted the trap.

- Open the door again from the outside. It will now remain open, even when you cross the trip wire.

- Go in and trip the boss into action. Pump a few RPG shots into him and run back into (35).

- Use the columns for cover, and make that bad boss pay the ultimate price for stealing our chicks. He's too big to fit through the door and too stupid or arrogant to run away from you. I told you his head was his weakest point.

After you've brought him down, let the animation sequence run (in other words, don't hit any keys). It's Duke-attitude at its best. Congratulations, you stud!

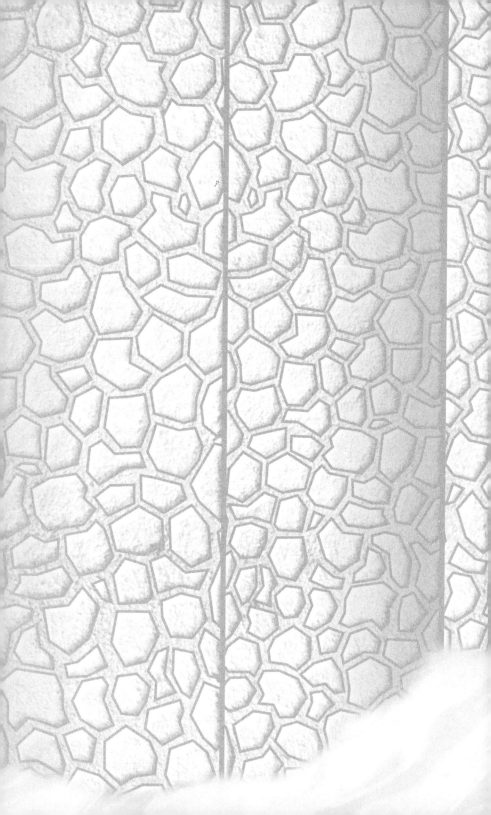

MISSION 6:
LAUNCH FACILITY

Don't be confused that this is called Mission 6. You can only access this mission from Mission 4. We suspect the game's designers created this while Mission Five was already underway.

Monikers aside, Mission 6 is a very straight-forward—if you made it through the Toxic Dump, you've seen 95 percent of this mission already.

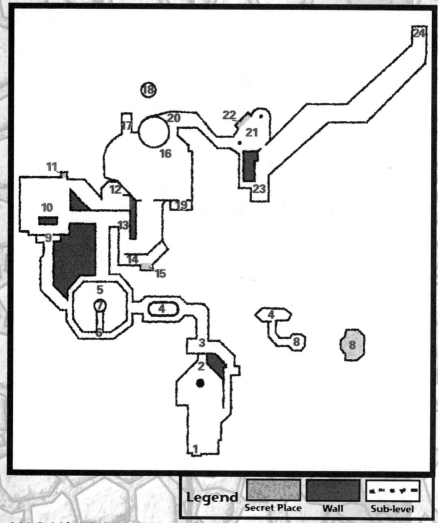

HIGHLIGHTS

- All four secret places
- Take some pigs to slaughter
- Destroy "Apollo 13" before it even leaves the launch pad

MISSION 6: LAUNCH FACILITY AT-A-GLANCE

1 Start, pistol, medkit, shotgun ammo
2 Switch to open (3)
3 Forcefield, boots, armor
4 Shotgun
5 Medkits, pistol ammo
6 Medkits, chaingun & ammo, button lock (* * * *)
7 Blue key, medkit, shotgun ammo, monitor, 01 switch
* **8** Healing Atoms, shotgun ammo
9 Forcefield switch, chaingun ammo, medkit, pipebombs, light switch
10 Healing Atom, medkit, shotgun ammo, RPG
***11** Pipebombs
12 Chaingun ammo, monitor, portable medkit, blue key lock
13 Shotgun ammo
14 Red key, shotgun ammo, switch, monitor
***15** Armor
16 Night vision goggles
17 Jet pack, teleporter (to 18), monitor
18 Cocoons, medkits, red key lock
19 Holoduke, steroids, shotgun & ammo, switch
20 Rocket carcass
21 Medkit, shotgun ammo, boots, switch
***22** Healing Atoms
23 Medkit
24 End

*Denotes secret place

Duke'm, We Have a Problem

1   Start.

2   Go down the ramp, and blast the Aliens that teleport in. Wade into the slime, venture behind the churn and hit the switch. It deactivates the forcefield at (3).

3   Open the panel. This also opens a wall behind you back down the hall from (2)—meaning you get attacked from behind by some crafty Aliens. Go back to get the armor in their room before going on to (4).

4   Go around the slime. If you need a shotgun, dive in. If you do dive in, note the grating—it'll drop after you nab the blue key at (6).

5   This is the level's central hub. Watch for turret fire. Note the door marked 01. Hmmmmm. . . .

6   Go up the ramp. The combination for the button puzzle at the top is: (* * * *).

7   Collect your swag. The blue key is behind the small red door. What do you wanna bet that the 01 switch is connected to the forcefield door called 01? But first, go back to (4) and jump in the slime. Swim through the now-opened passage.

8   Secret place. Collect your stuff, go back to (5) and through the now-open 01 forcefield.

9   Two alcoves at the top of the ramp hide some Aliens and high explosives. The switch in the right alcove sheds light into (10).

10 Just so you know, when you leap onto the raised platform for the Healing Atom you don't trigger an Alien attack. If you can make the jump, it's yours. Note the locked door to your right—the blue key card opens it. To get to that elusive blue key lock, go up the ramp on the left that curls around the room.

11 Secret place. Shoot out the fan above you. You have to jet pack up to the ledge with the pipebombs. You'll take damage if you don't safely jet pack down to the ramp.

12 The alcove to the left contains the blue key lock. This opens the door into (13). You overlook area (16) from here. Go back down the ramp and through (10).

13 The doors you see before you lead you up to the computer loft (14). From the corner, launch an RPG round into the loft. Ahhh, the sweet smell of seared hog flesh.

14 Grab the red key—it fits in Apollo's control module (18). Hit the button switch to open the large blue doors dead ahead—to (16).

15 Secret place. The armor is located behind the third full panel on the right—as you enter (14).

16 Make no mistake, this is a big one. Go to the square patch of light to the left of the rocket and hit [Spacebar]. Going up. Note the large, low, red rectangle to your right. That's (19).

17 The teleport takes you to the command module. Step in now, Duke.

18 What's this? Those Alien maggots were on chicks! Do what you must to the chicks, insert the red key card, then teleport back to (17) and ride down the elevator.

19 Duck into the red alcove. The red key primed the knife switch inside. Hit it. Holy. . . . Go through the now-opened red door across from you. It's an elevator—going down.

20 The remains of the rocket are to your left. Crawl on it like a little kid, if you want, but there's nothing there except maybe a few lurking Aliens.

21 Clean out the Alien menace. The switch to the left of the computer bank opens a panel directly behind you. A few well-placed RPG shots make mincemeat out of those Aliens.

22 Secret place. Leap onto computer panel and hit [Spacebar]. Heal thyself!

23 Leap into the slime river and ride it to the nuke badge at (24).

24 That's it for Episode One, Dukeboy.

CHAPTER 5

EPISODE TWO LUNAR APOCALYPSE

Episode Two begins the meat of the *Duke Nukem* experience, and that's a good thing.

Chicks are being off-loaded at an alarming rate, and it's up to Duke Nukem to put a crimp in the style of the other-world scum.

There are new bad guys aplenty—Enforcers, Assault Commanders and Protozoid Slimers—and a disturbing amount of Boss Monsters akin to the space ape at the end of Episode One. There are also new weapons to play with; some better than others, but all worth a squeeze of the trigger.

The missions tend to fluctuate in intensity, without a clear progression of difficulty, so don't get discouraged if you struggle through a scenario or two. And the secret missions...well, let's just say that ammo conservation is not a key tactic.

The walk-through that follows will take you everywhere, and accomplish everything, without cheat codes or the use of God Mode. The right choice of weaponry is crucial, since not all ammo is as plentiful as others. Even if you don't follow along room by room, read the brief summary that begins each mission for hints on proper resource management.

Now pick up that damn pistol and head for the moon, Duke Nukem. There's a load of scum up there just begging to be reckoned with.

MISSION 1: SPACEPORT

Now that Duke has an idea of the Alien's putrid plan—namely, offloading chicks at an alarming rate—he's gone lunar to make those bastards pay.

In the first mission of Episode Two, Nukem confronts the otherworldly horde as he arrives on the moon, clearing our spaceport of an infestation most vile. Along the way, you get to pick up some trick new devices—namely the Shrinker and the Devastator—and test them on a few new scumbags to boot.

As chick transports hurry through the inky void, Duke does what comes natural—raining death and destruction at an ever-increasing pace. Contrary to Sammy Hagar's assertion, there may be more than one way to rock...but Duke knows them all, and demonstrates each with authority.

HIGHLIGHTS

- Six secret places
- Two new enemies: The Enforcer and the Sentry Drone
- Two new weapons: The Devastator and the Shrinker

Mission 1: Spaceport At-a-Glance

1 Teleporter
2 Steroids, RPG
3 Shotgun, medkit, switch to forcefield
* 4 Healing Atom
* 5 RPG ammo
6 Drinking fountain
7 Medkit
* 8 RPG ammo
9 Blue key, portable medkit, pistol ammo, armor, scuba gear
10 Chaingun cannon, night vision goggles
11 RPG ammo, medkit
12 Shotgun ammo, Holoduke, blue key lock
13 Medkit, shotgun ammo, pistol ammo, jet pack, Healing Atom
*14 Chaingun ammo
15 Shotgun ammo, switch to combination panel in room (16).
16 Pipebombs, button puzzle (* * * *)
*17 Devastator, Healing Atom, night vision goggles, medkit
18 Red key, Healing Atoms, jet pack
19 Elevator, red key lock
*20 Shrinker, armor, medkits
21 Sentry Drone ambush, end

*Denotes secret place

Screams in Space

1 Once you've verbalized the penalty for chick stealing, step into the teleporter behind you for a quick trip to the nearby spaceship. Note that if you linger too long near any of the windows in the spaceport, a passing chick transport won't hesitate to get in a cheap shot.

2 In the ship are steroids and an RPG, as well as a desperate message from Earth and a little reading material.

3 Turn to your right as you enter this area and dispose of the Aliens. Near the control console is a shotgun and a medkit, as well as the switch which drops the forcefield to the restricted area. To open the first secret place of Episode Two, search the control panel near the shotgun.

4 Secret place. An Alien guards a Healing Atom, but not for long. To reach the second secret place in the vicinity, double back to where the hallway enters this room and approach the video monitor. As you do, a panel above and behind you slides open.

5 Secret place. With your back to the video screen, it's easy to run and jump to this area, and claim the RPG ammo.

6 Drop the Alien in the hallway and pause at the drinking fountain if you need a health boost.

7 More Alien scum. Send them to hell, and grab the large medkit off the floor near the window. Secret place numero tres is located above and to the right of the entryway where the Aliens once stood. Jump up and you'll pass right through the "authorized personnel" sign.

8 Secret place. Collect the RPG ammo, and drop into the shaft where the light flickers nearby. Follow the vent shaft to (9), kicking out the vent for access.

9 Mega-goodies, including the blue key, a portable medkit, pistol ammo, armor, and scuba gear. Watch out, an Enforcer will drop from the ceiling to rip into you as you approach the ramp leading up to (11). Two more Enforcers lurk in (11), and a wise Duke would peg them through the connecting window.

10 Howzabout a little space scuba? As you dive, collect a chain-gun and night vision goggles.

11 If you thinned out the crowd by blasting through the window of room (9), you only have Aliens to deal with now. Otherwise, a pair of Enforcers add to your woe. Clean house, and collect RPG ammo and a medkit, as well as whatever the Enforcers were packing. The ramp to the left of the alcove above leads back to (7), while the elevator upstairs lies on the opposite side. Punish the Alien that rides down to greet you, and head upstairs.

12 Check the monitor and collect the shotgun ammo. The right-hand picture of Earth slides to reveal a Holoduke, after which you should ceremoniously insert the blue key into the nearby lock. The key lock opens the door at the far end of (11), and unleashes an Enforcer goon squad. The elevator the goons were standing in rises to room (13).

13 This large area is full of goodies, and, unfortunately, Enforcers. A medkit and ammo for both the shotgun and pistol lie nearby; and, by jumping atop the box, you can reach an alcove that hides a jet pack. Once you've strapped on the pack, you can hover up and get the Healing Atom, and visit a secret place. Detonating the gas canisters unleashes another Enforcer, and opens up a hole in the wall to (14).

14 Secret place. When you pick up the Healing Atom, a door opens in room (11). 'Roid and run for chaingun ammo.

15 Detonate the canisters for entry, and watch your back. Shotgun shells await, as well as a switch that reveals a button puzzle in (16).

16 An Alien dirtbag desperately defends a stash of pipebombs and the aforementioned puzzle. Changing the position of the two center buttons drops the red forcefield outside. The final combo looks like this: * * * *. Now, return to room (13) and jet pack the inoperable elevator shaft.

17 Secret place. Kill the Enforcer, strap on the Devastator and utilize the nearby Healing Atom. Don't forget to check up top for a medkit and night vision goggles. To exit, drop down the large orange opening in the floor. You'll fall all the way through rooms (13) and (11), and plunge underwater.

> ## Tip!
>
> The Devastator is appropriately named, but it comes with a couple of cautions. First, it's easy to go through ammo at an astonishing rate, and it's not really necessary. Keep your finger light on the trigger. Also, as with the RPG, make sure you have a good gap between Duke and his intended target, or you'll feel the heat as well.

18 Grab the red key. Pushing the button on the wall opens a panel with Healing Atoms and another jet pack. Several more Enforcers are also unleashed, so be prepared to fight your way back to (16) and the large door therein.

19 Clear the hallway of Enforcers. Stand in the lighted section of the hall, and hit the [Spacebar]; you'll trigger an elevator. Going down!

20 Secret place. An Enforcer makes a stand between you and the Shrinker. Armor and medkits also lie nearby. The shaft in the wall holds another medkit, en route back to room (16). Ride the elevator back up and use that key on the panel in (19) instead.

> ## Tip!
>
> The Shrinker is pure Duke fun. Unleash on your victim and then chase them down to apply the boot...where's a doormat when you need one?

21 Jump back quick and hammer the Sentry Drone; if it can, it'll fly right into you and explode. Not very sporting, is it? End.

MISSION 2: INCUBATOR

There could be worse things than the disgusting little mission dubbed Incubator—like maybe enduring a marathon of showtunes with your head in a vice—still, Duke has got a job to do, and scum waits for no one.

  As Duke exterminates vermin and puts chicks out of their misery, he also has a new foe, a new weapon in store, and the biggest crowd of Octabrains to date assembled in one locale. This mission is a small one, in a spatial sense, but taxing in the extreme when it comes to combat. Keep your wits about you, and let God sort them out....

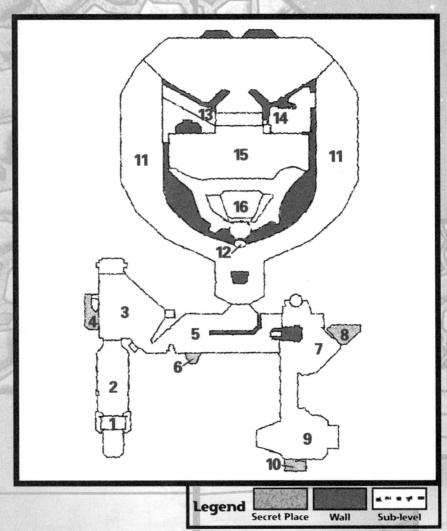

HIGHLIGHTS

- Five secret places
- One new enemy: The Protozoid Slimer
- One hot new weapon: The Freezethrower

MISSION 2: INCUBATOR AT-A-GLANCE

    1 Shotgun, medkit
    2 Turret gun
    3 Shotgun ammo, chaingun ammo, two medkits, pipebombs, Healing Atom, night vision goggles.
* * 4 Armor, shotgun ammo
    5 Crest, secured door
* 6 Portable medkit.
    7 Pistol ammo, shotgun ammo, laser tripbombs
* 8 Holoduke, Freezethrower
    9 Healing Atoms, switch
*10 Chaingun ammo
  11 Medkit
  12 RPG, shotgun ammo, chaingun ammo
  13 Yellow key
  14 Yellow key lock, pistol, switch
  15 Medkit, RPG ammo, shotgun ammo, Freezethrower ammo, portable medkit, steroids, Devastator and ammo, pipebombs, Shrinker, jet pack, switch
  16 End

    *Denotes secret place

TURNING UP THE HEAT

1   Before venturing further, you can grab the shotgun out of the panel on your left and the small medkit on the floor.

2   Dispatch the three Sentry Drones in the hallway, and proceed with caution: Above the door, as you enter, is a turret gun ready to open up Duke's backside.

3   Three Enforcers guard this control center, which has several goodies in plain sight as well some not-so-obvious hidden treasures. Take care of the welcoming committee, and acquire the shotgun ammo, chaingun ammo, and two large medkits.

    Behind a panel, just past the large console, is a cache of pipebombs; and if you hop inside that small area, you'll discover it has a false wall at the rear, leading to a secret place.

    Throwing the switch between the double doors opens an alcove above and to your right, unleashing a swarm of Sentry Drones, as well as opening up both large doors—which are actually windows, revealing a Gieger-esque infection on the outer hull. Also, another smaller door, near where you first entered, opens when the switch is thrown. A prudent Duke might lace the area in front of the Drone alcove with pipebombs to help soften the arriving opposition.

    In the Drone alcove is a Healing Atom, and a panel to the right of the small door (the one opened by the wall switch) contains night vision goggles.

4   Secret places. Behind the large control panel is a room containing a monitor, as well as armor and shells for the ever-lovin' shotgun. Note that the room actually gives the "Secret Place" message twice. Activating the monitor pays homage to George Lucas' first film.

5   Aliens lurk hereabouts, and if that big crest on the wall caught your eye, it's probably for a reason....

6   Secret place. Behind the crest lies a portable medkit.

7   Climbing the ramp outside opens the door to this room. Inside are several items (including laser tripbombs), an Alien with a distinctly hostile nature, and a secret place—

behind one of the large computer panels to the right of the armory.

> ### Note!
> The tripbomb contributes a new level of cunning to Duke attacks. Simply slap it on a flat surface, and the device automatically activates after a couple of seconds, sending a familiar red beam across any portal. When tripped, the bomb detonates in the direction of your hapless victim. Pain and death ensue.

8   Secret place. Expect a sneak attack from behind—an Enforcer and an Alien—when you enter this room. Punish the vermin and celebrate: here's Holoduke and another new toy, the Freezethrower.

> ### Note!
> The Freezethrower adds a new dimension to Dukedom, crystallizing your enemies in a flash of nitrogen. One swift kick to an adversary thus affected has shattering results, but if you hesitate too long you'll allow the scum to thaw.

9   Climbing the ramp to this room, hug the left-hand wall and equip the RPG. Don't be distracted by the three Aliens that rise from the floor to greet you: The real threat is a ceiling-mounted laser cannon, above and to your right as you enter. Grabbing the Healing Atoms unleashes Aliens and Sentry Drones, and standing too long in the atoms' alcove has a decidedly unhealthy effect. The wall switch near the monitor...hey, see if you can figure this one out for yourself, alright?

10 Secret place. This secret place contains ordinary old chain-gun ammo. Smile when you say that, Duke.

11 Expect an Enforcer ambush as you approach the UNsecured area. Near the armory cowers an Alien, and he's not the only local in need of an artillery overdose. In the hallways left and

right, dispense justice upon: an Octabrain; several Protozoid Slimers, and/or their pods; Sentry Drones; and a chick in need of sweet release. One small medkit awaits.

12 In the Armory, collect an RPG cannon, as well as ammo for the shotgun and chaingun.

13 At the end of the left hall is a hidden alcove with the yellow key, and a locked door that provides a peek at things to come.

14 Circling around to the hallway opposite the location of the yellow key—waddaya know, the yellow key lock. Enforcers object to your intrusion, but then off world scum always seem to resent a hero right before their death. Watch for the ceiling-mounted laser turret, and pick off as many pods as you can from here. Take the pistol off the control console and shoot the switch. Now, when you exit back into the hallway, you'll find that the wall to your left has dropped to allow you entrance. The corresponding section of wall at the end of the other hallway also dropped, and the jail door near where you found the yellow key is now open. A Sentry Drone patrols the other hallway, just in case your partial to that approach.

15 Whichever means of entrance you choose to this large area, expect to be battling Slimers constantly. More useful points of interest include:

- a large medkit and ammo for both the RPG and the shotgun in the areas near where each hall dropped to allow your entry;

- ammo for the Freezer on the walkway between the bodies of water, and also among the chicks;

- a portable medkit and steroids behind the first aid panel at one end of the walkway;

- a veritable Octabrain party beneath the waves in the direction of the chicks: Drop Holoduke while you clear the area of Slimers, then let the Octas eat RPG. In the underwater caves are another Devastator weapon and ammo;

- an alcove high on the wall, complete with a laser turret and a panel concealing pipebombs; plenty o' chicks in various stages of duress, whose demise ushers in Aliens;

- more octas, another Shrinker, and a jet pack in the hall-way above the chicks; and,

- a small switch low and to the left as you face the cliffs that unleashes another horde of Octabrains, which has been merrily guarding a pod field.

16 The end-of-the-level switch is under the supervision of still more Octabrains. Punch that sucker and get the hell out of here.

MISSION 3: WARP FACTOR

The Warp Factor mission is not without a certain charm...it certainly has a familiar silhouette. It also has more Sentry Drones than you can shake an RPG at, and a trio of brutal baddies waiting at the end.

You'll want to be relatively conservative with certain types of ammo. Shotgun shells are hard to come by, though you could freeze more meat than Tyson Foods and still have cartridges to spare. Also, be mindful of dispensing too much Devastator fire until near the end of the mission. It'll come in handy; trust us.

If you're ready, Captain Duke...if you're REALLY ready...yeah, it's kind of an inside joke. You'll get it before the level's through, assuming you know your *Next Generation* at all.

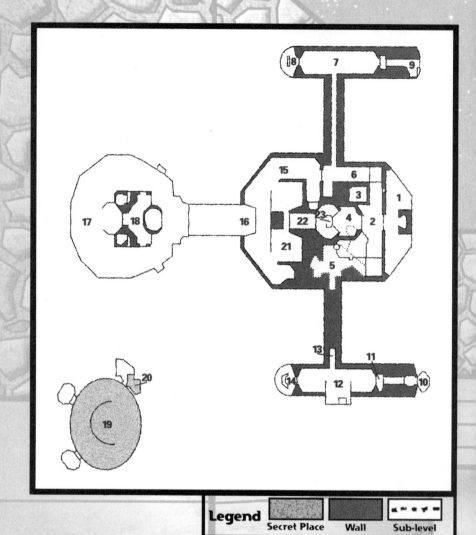

HIGHLIGHTS

- Two secret places
- One new enemy: The Assault Commander
- Drones, Drones, and more Drones

MISSION 3: WARP FACTOR AT-A-GLANCE

1 Chaingun, medkit
2 RPG ammo, pipebombs, Freezethrower
3 Shotgun shells, portable medkit
4 Pistol, chaingun ammo, medkit
5 Medkits, pistol ammo, Healing Atom, shotgun, armor, laser tripbomb, blue key
6 Medkit, blue key lock
7 Medkit
8 Devastator ammo
9 Medkit, chaingun ammo
10 Medkits
11 Devastator ammo
12 Yellow key, shotgun ammo, Shrinker ammo, medkits
13 Healing Atoms
14 RPG
15 Shotgun ammo, Shrinker, yellow key lock
16 Shrinker ammo
17 Devastator, portable medkit, five medkits, steroids, switch, Freezethrower ammo
18 Switch, RPG, Holoduke
*19 RPG, pipebombs, Healing Atom, chaingun, portable medkit
*20 Freezethrower, Devastator
21 Shotgun, pistol ammo, medkit
22 Radiation room
23 Medkits, end

*Denotes secret place

AN ENTERPRISING DUKE

1 The first room of this level can literally be a pain. Four Sentry Drones wait just outside the initial chamber, and dealing with them while not taking significant damage is as much luck as skill. Try moving all the way to the right of the portal you face as the level begins, and chaingunning the first Drone (to the left) before it can close the gap. The trick is not to activate the Drone on your right at the same time. Two more Drones wait out of view. To your right is a chaingun, and at the far left is a small medkit.

2 This large area has plenty to see and do:

   ☞ Six more Drones wait in stasis inside room (3). The door rises when you move in the direction of the armory on your left, so be prepared to unload serious firepower in the Drones' direction.

   ☞ In the armory itself is RPG ammo, and you'll be bum rushed from behind by an Enforcer when you open the armory door.

   ☞ In the wall panel to your right as you enter the room are pipebombs.

   ☞ Behind a wall panel near the armory is another Freezethrower.

   ☞ The large dead-end hallways to the left and right are elevators down, each with it's own unique trap. The one on the left causes a serious series of explosions as it descends, and you take big time damage unless you activate it (simply step over the threshold) and quickly step back into this room. The elevator on the right drops to a hallway where two Enforcers wait. They rush forward when they see you and set off several trip-bombs. Ride down, and when you have the Enforcers attention, ride right back up again—they'll still trip the trap, but you won't be around to absorb the intended punishment.

3 The room that housed the dirty half-dozen Drones holds shotgun shells and a portable medkit.

4 Two Aliens teleport in to defend a pistol, chaingun ammo and a small medkit. In case you're wondering, curious Duke, the end of this level lies at the heart of the reactor. You can only gain access to the reactor's core from the opposite direction.

5 Scour this large area, now ruins, for Alien scum, large medkits, pistol ammo, an Healing Atom (Note: Only one atom is available to you now. You have to take the shuttle to get beyond the barrier, where you can see more Atoms just out of reach, and that train doesn't stop here.), a shotgun, armor, a laser tripbomb and the blue key (Note: To exit the key area, you must squat and then stand upright close to the fire. You'll simply pop right out.)

6 Usually, one of the Enforcers will still be in business after the other was tripbombed into oblivion. Put the straggler out of commission. There's a large medkit near the blue key lock.

7 Open the final elevator door ready for business: A swarm of Sentry Drones patrols the tunnel beyond. A small medkit lies near the door you should open first, just in case you needed that.

8 Two more Enforcers await a quick death herein. Scoop up the Devastator ammo and check the monitor for a cool outside view of the spacestation (gee; it doesn't look anything like the U.S.S. Enterprise—copyright lawyers can be so intimidating). Also under surveillance: the aforementioned shuttle, presided over by an Alien escort. Time to go show them your ticket to ride.

9 Enforcers and Sentry Drones bar your way, and isn't that Drone-in-a-tunnel thing starting to get a little old? Gobble the small medkit and check behind the shuttle switch for more chaingun ammo. Flip the switch and pay the Aliens the required fare. Another will teleport in after you board.

10 Dispatch the Alien and scarf a couple more small medkits.

11 This small antechamber holds Devastator ammo.

12 Prepare to be Droned when you pop the hatch to this area.... Also in attendance are a gaggle of Aliens with a serious deathwish problem. The yellow key is inside the cylinder. Pressing the center button on the console swings open the

doors for access, but the doors will swing closed again. There's a switch inside the chamber to let you back out. Nearby, you'll also collect Shotgun ammo, Shrinker ammo, and medkits.

13 In need, Dukester? Ride down the elevator and claim those previously sighted Healing Atoms—there are three.

14 Two Enforcers guard an RPG, briefly. Stepping into the room also triggers the arrival of a Drone and three more Enforcers behind you. The party gets crowded in a hurry, but be a gracious host, Duke—there's always room for death. Try lacing the passageway with pipebombs, then backing into the room once the first Enforcer has been dealt with. When the scum show up to jump you from behind, detonate the pipes with an RPG blast. Game, set, match: Duke. Watch out for any lurking stragglers when you venture back into the hallway—they'll hide behind the walls on the right. Count on more Enforcer and Drone trouble as you make your way back towards the next room.

15 Expect an Alien ambush when you step into this room. Raising the tactical display, with the switch on the nearby console, grants you more shotgun ammo, and there's another Shrinker behind a false wall in the darkened area.

Once the initial threat is dealt with, there are a bevy of major badasses just up ahead: A monster akin to the boss at the end of Episode One, and also a putrid pair of Assault Commanders in hideous hovercars.

The first monster comes into view as you round the corner of the large hallway. Stop and dispatch him from there, or you'll trigger the Assault Commander to attack from a room on your left. Hopefully, you've taken our advice and saved up on Devastator ammo. It's time to dispense it liberally.

The Assault Commanders are a pain in the ass if they get the drop on you, but they can be shrunk, whereupon they become about as intimidating as gnats. If you rush past the entrance to their area, they won't see you; and since the room they're guarding is also protected by a forcefield that you have to deactivate from afar, skip them for now, if possible. Use the yellow key on the panel where the first monster stood, and proceed with caution.

16 Kill the two Enforcers and take the Shrinker ammo before heading up the ramp.

17 As you circle to the back of this area, you'll be beset by a swarm of Drones, and fired upon by a ceiling-mounted laser turret. Through the door, directly in front of you as you enter, is an unguarded Devastator, yours for the taking. Other items of interest include:

☞ portable medkit, behind the clearly marked panel to your right as you enter: Don't use it yet, weary Dukeman! There are five large medkits nearby;

☞ a dose of steroids, behind the lit section of wall on your right just past the aforementioned medkit: A switch on the wall in this alcove leads to this mission's only two secret places...for now, clear the immediate area. The switch will still be there when you've disposed of the local riffraff;

☞ ammo for the Freezethrower, atop the console on the left past where you picked up the 'roids: note that from this position, you can lob a few pipebombs into the clearing—not too far—and bait the first two Drones to their doom by sticking your nose out a little further;

☞ two large medkits, in the area up the ramp where the Drones were waiting. Pushing the switch here sheds some light on the surroundings, courtesy of mother earth; and,

☞ three more large medkits, lying near the wall to your left as you circle past the ramp.

18 Inside this room are a pair of Enforcers, as well as the switch controlling the forcefield near those Assault Commanders. Another Drone and an Enforcer were released outside when you started poking around, and the Drone will get the drop on you if you're not careful. Aside from the obvious entrances to this room, you can slide away an adjoining wall between here and the globe area, above where you find the RPG—the Drone has been known to take advantage of that fact. The large panel of the circular control center slides to unveil yer ol' buddy, Holoduke.

19 Secret place. On the bridge, you'll find an RPG, pipebombs, a Healing Atom, a chaingun, and zero enemy resistance. Once you enter the conference room, however, things take a nasty turn. An entire posse of Drones and Enforcers attempts to confer with you in unpleasant terms as soon as you venture inside. Try mining the area near the conference room door with pipebombs, then setting up a tripbomb in the doorway. Take up a position near the window and RPG the livin' hell out of anything that survives your initial trap. Inside the conference room is a portable medkit, and by pressing on the back of the laptop, you open the door to a second secret place.

20 Secret place. Yes, it's the REALLY Ready Room, complete with Freezethrower, Devastator, and porn. Maneuvering near the chick flicks will give the secret place message.

21 Shrink the Assault Commanders down to a manageable size, and be wary of Drones and Enforcers in the vicinity. Don't forget to grab that shotgun from the niche in the rock wall outside. There's also pistol ammo and a small medkit in the room proper.

22 Hurry through the blue room or you'll suffer a nasty radiation burn. Wait at the door for the rotating wall sections to reveal the central core, 'roid up, run over, and ride down.

23 Dispatch the Enforcers and get healthy. The mission ending switch is nearby.

MISSION 4: FUSION STATION

The Fusion Station is a relatively new look for Duke Nukem, as the entire level is comprised of one huge structure, and for the most part, entire floors of the reactor facility are confronted at once. Lots of gang-tackling ahead, and the proverbial buttload of Assault Commanders.

At the end of this level is another somewhat unique occurrence, in that you actually have a huge area wherein to fight a flock of Assault Commanders—if that's your cup of tea. Personally, it takes a glutton for punishment to fight a Commander on his terms: It's much better to get in close—so they ignore their missiles—and shrink them down to size.

This mission starts off tame, but by the end you'll be ready for a breather; and no matter how long it is until you see one of those fatsos floating your way again, it'll be too soon.

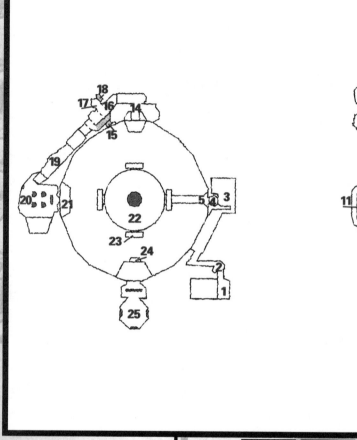

Legend Secret Place Wall Sub-level

HIGHLIGHTS

- Seven secret places
- Far too many Assault Commanders
- One big, badass nuclear reactor

MISSION 4: FUSION STATION AT-A-GLANCE

1 Medkit
2 Shotgun
3 RPG, RPG ammo, medkit, Healing Atom, armor
4 Drone ambush
5 Pistol
6 Two medkits, laser tripbombs, pistol ammo, two boxes of shotgun ammo, protective boots
7 Portable medkit, chaingun
* 8 Chaingun ammo
* 9 Medkit
*10 Pipebombs
11 Healing Atoms, switch
12 Chaingun ammo, pipebombs, medkits, switches, shotgun ammo
*13 Freezethrower ammo
14 Shrinker
15 Armor
16 Medkits
17 Healing Atom
18 RPG ammo
19 Tripbombs, medkit
20 Devastator, shotgun ammo, steroids, medkits, switch
21 Devastator ammo
22 Devastator ammo, RPG ammo, and medkit
23 Portable medkit, shotgun, Devastator ammo
24 Healing Atoms, jet pack
25 Chaingun, Healing Atom, end

*Denotes secret place

THE CORE OF THE PROBLEM

1   Drop the Alien that welcomes you to the Fusion Station. A large medkit lies nearby, just in case you didn't get your fill in the final room of Mission 3.

2   Grant the chick's last wish and claim the shotgun behind her pod. An Octabrain hears the commotion and investigates, much to his regret.

3   More Aliens beg for death as you traverse this winding hallway. Take care of the laser turrets that blast through the window slit on your left; in the room where the hallway terminates, you can pick up an RPG and some ammo, as well as a large medkit. When you search the wall panel, near the monitor, the column in the center of the room rises to reveal a Healing Atom. Check that monitor for a glimpse of things to come, and don't forget the armor on the windowsill behind you.

4   Kill the Alien in the antechamber to this room, and approach the door with caution. A Drone waits on the other side, and the door may open automatically to allow it a cheap shot.

5   Pick up the pistol to your right. Aren't you glad you already polished off those turrets? If you're still packing a jet pack, you could alight on any of the nearby landings, but all points hereabouts are accessible through the central core...might as well send the otherworld scum to hell in the order that God intended.

6   Ride the elevator down and clear out the lower level of Enforcers. In addition to whatever the body count yields, you should also collect: two large medkits; three laser trip-bombs; pistol ammo, two boxes of shotgun ammo, and protective boots.

7   If you hop up next to the huge pistons of the machine, you'll find a portable medkit. Drop inside one of the pistons nearest the elevator which you rode down, and you'll find a small network of tunnels. In the area between the pistons, at that end of the machine, rests a chaingun. Search the wall opposite the small tunnel to discover a secret place.

8   Secret place. A goodly stash of chaingun ammo.

9   Secret place. Search the ledge opposite the elevator you arrived on, and gain access to a hall, a pod, and a large medkit.

10 Secret place. In the same direction as the medkit, turn left and jump up at the end of the hall for serious pipebombs.

11 Backtrack to the end of the hall opposite the pipebombs to claim the Healing Atoms you could see from (7). The switch opens another elevator door in the room outside.

12 Slay the enforcers, ride the elevator up to the next level of the reactor, and take out still more scum. There's plenty of chaingun ammo nearby, even if the freaks don't drop a round. Strap on the scuba gear, collect the two boxes of pipebombs, and a large medkit. Throw both switches in the small underwater alcoves and surface on the other side of the room. Alien scum will offer to towel you off: refuse in no uncertain terms, collect the shotgun ammo and any medkits that might appeal to you, then check the monitor to reveal a secret place.

13 Secret place. Moving near the monitor opens a small room to the right of the exit door. Inside lies Freezethrower ammo.

14 When the door opens, you're back outside again, looking across at a landing flanked by two window slits. Lob a couple RPGs to soften up the Aliens, then shoot the switch to summon the taxi. Inside the room are pods galore and a chick in dire straits. Easing her pain evokes an Octabrain sneak attack. On the floor nearby is a Shrinker. In the alcove opposite where the chick was cocooned, just to the right of that other window slit, is a panel in the wall.

15 Secret place. Raise the column and claim the armor.

16 Dispatch the Enforcers in the hallway and proceed with caution. About a third of the way down you'll trigger a nasty chain of explosions, and it would be wise to duck back near the door you just came through and ride it out. Another Enforcer will arrive about then. On the floor near ground zero is a large medkit, and another lies at the far end of the hall.

    As you stride down the hall, take a minute to visit two more secret places. Simply step into the fissure on your right, and climb to the top of the overpass. Do you see the opening across the way, where it looks like a fan blew out?

17 Secret place. This pod filled hallway is indeed a secret place. Paint it red, and watch for the Enforcer. Another chick needs your gentle touch, and a Healing Atom is your reward. Note the crack in the wall to her right.

18 Secret place. Blowing open the wall nets a box of RPG ammo and another secret place message. Note that while you were wreaking havoc, another Enforcer showed up down below. Stand on the overpass nearest the door and fish with pipebombs if he hasn't come looking for you yet.

19 An Enforcer patrols the bridge leading to this room. Once you've paid the toll in lead, flip a pipebomb through the portal and stand back. Inside, the gas canisters make quick work of the Sentry's chums, and also open a hole in the wall to reveal a pair of laser tripbombs. There's also a large med-kit nearby, and a couple more Enforcers waiting to jump your back as you approach the far door.

20 Ride the elevator up and waste some more scum—for Enforcers, these punks are really lacking. In the center of the room is a Devastator weapon; and as you circle, the wall fur-thest from where you enter blows open to emit more losers. Be ready with that RPG. Inside the room are shotgun shells, steroids and a large medkit. There's also a large medkit to the left of the next door, which opens momentarily when you throw the wall switch in the room where that last batch of Enforcers was hiding. 'Roid up and run, but be careful not to go too far.

21 You exit the last room onto a platform, and must deal immediately with onrushing Drones and Alien marksmen. A box of Devastator ammo lies nearby. Once the firefight has died down, small pun intended, ride across the chasm via the time-honored switch shot.

22 The upper level of the central core is a happy little place indeed. First off, you'll want to shoulder your projectile weapons—use either the Shrinker or the Freezethrower for the initial confrontation. Yes, we'll explain why.

As you enter, the huge column in the room will descend, cutting loose several Enforcers in your direction. A gigantic electrical arc erupts between the pit that the column sank into and the ceiling; and if you strike anywhere in that vicinity with a projectile, you'll unleash a hellish series of explosions. Stomp the Enforcers, then skirt the perimeter to collect copious amounts of ammo for the Devastator and RPG, as well as a large medkit.

When all the goodies are in your possession, flip a pipebomb into the arc and duck back out to the landing before you detonate. Yes, that gravelly voice you hear is another Assault Commander. Give him something to suck on, and proceed through the hole blown in the nearby door.

23 Ride the elevator up and exult in the booty: a portable medkit, shotgun, and a couple more boxes of Devastator ammo. Another ledge, another...what the hell? Where's the convenient skycart? Looking across at the other landing, direct your gaze downward about 50 meters (relatively speaking). On the ledge below lies a pair of Healing Atoms and a jet pack, just in case you've already spent your fuel. Time for a little dogfighting, Dukestyle.

24 A running jump will net you the pack and boost your health considerably. Unfortunately, when you alight on the platform in front of the far door, a swarm of Assault Commanders is unleashed. Fortunately, you've got plenty of wide open spaces, as well as ammo, right stud? Give the bloated floaters whatfor, preferably without letting them escape from the alcove.

25 Inside, two more Assault Commanders guard a couple of chicks, as well as a chaingun and a Healing Atom. Lure the Commanders out of the room one at a time if you can, and shrink them before they begin to fight. Killing the babes ushers in Octabrains, and alighting on the platform where the chicks are cocooned causes the pillar in the center of the room to open. Inside is one last Assault Commander, and the end-of-the-level switch.

MISSION 5: OCCUPIED TERRITORY

Occupied Territory is just that: Filled to the hilt with scum, all of whom are looking for trouble. Assault Commanders? Hey, those guys are sissys. Remember the Boss Monster that concludes Episode One? There are five on this mission, and none of them go out of their way to be cuddly.

Hang onto RPG and Devastator ammo as if it were a gift from God. You're going to need every bit of it to get through the last few rooms here, though there is a pipebomb alternative we're quite proud of....

Grab that chaingun and buckle up, Dukeman. It's time to clear out the Occupied Territory.

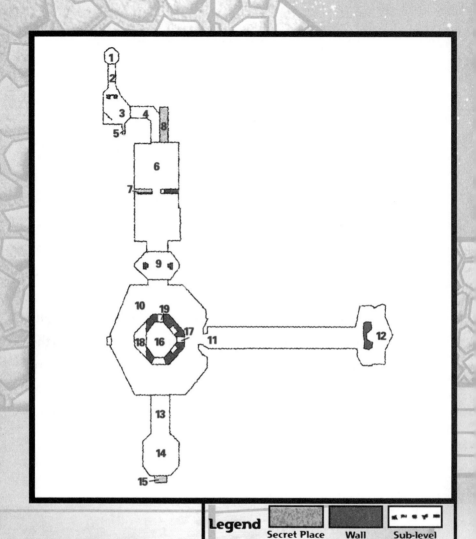

| Legend | Secret Place | Wall | Sub-level |

HIGHLIGHTS

- Four secret places
- Five Boss Monsters
- No vacancies

MISSION 5: OCCUPIED TERRITORY AT-A-GLANCE

1 Shotgun ammo, switch

2 Medkit

3 Pistol clips, chaingun, armor, portable medkit, switch

4 Hallway

* 5 Healing Atom

6 Medkit, chaingun ammo, Devastator ammo, night vision goggles, Holoduke, RPG ammo, Healing Atom

* 7 RPG, armor

* 8 Healing Atom, RPG ammo

9 Medkits

10 Medkit, steroids

11 Shrinker ammo

12 Pipebombs, Devastator, night vision goggles, red key

13 Devastator ammo

14 Blue key, medkit, chaingun ammo

*15 Tripbombs, Healing Atom

16 RPG ammo, portable medkit

17 Devastator ammo, medkit, switch

18 Medkit, end

19 Secret mission: Spin Cycle

*Denotes secret place

CREATING A VACANCY

1   Collect the shotgun and shells from the floor nearby. The switch on the wall behind you opens the doors to Occupied Territory.

2   Blast the pods and slay the babe, as well as the Octabrain that arrives thereafter. A large medkit lies on the floor nearby. As you cross the threshold to the next room the huge doors to your left seal. Don't sweat it.

3   Blast the Alien bastards through the window slit. On the floor nearby is a pistol clip, and in the niche, a chaingun. There's also armor in plain sight. Buttonhook around to your right to access the Aliens' area: Inside is a portable medkit, more pistol ammo, and the switch to those huge doors. Check the monitor for a preview.

4   An Enforcer goon squad begs for dismemberment when you open the doors to this hallway. Oblige them, but pause before proceeding to bask in the atomic glow of this mission's first secret place.

5   Secret place. Kneel down and look to your right at the giant doorway: inside the secret place is a Healing Atom.

6   This large room is merciless. When you enter, Assault Commanders on the far landing unload on you, and once you venture inside the room, an Enforcer joins the fray to add to your misery. Try taking up a position on one of the sloping panels to the left; there's another Assault Commander inside the room's second chamber, above and to the left. If you move to the right in that first chamber, the Assault Commander you can't see initially will take potshots at you. Kill the Enforcer first, then draw the Commanders out and shrink them down to size. As soon as you step on the ramp leading up to that far landing, a swarm of Drones pours out of the wall near where you came in. Keep moving, and pat yourself on yer little Duke butt when you finally survive. Load up, and don't forget Holoduke in the wall panel.

7   Secret place. When you enter the room's second segment, turn right and hug the wall. At the top of that ramp is a grate. Blow it out, and in the vent shaft you'll discover an RPG and armor.

8 Secret Place. The room the Drones rushed out of holds a Healing Atom and RPG ammo.

9 Dispense the three punk Aliens that guard two large med-kits.

10 Opening the door to this huge area is sure to get the attention of the Enforcer and the trio of Alien scum nearby. If you back into the room you just came from, they'll come and open up the door again to be greeted on your terms. Working your way around the core's perimeter, expect resistance from Aliens, Enforcers, and Drones. You should also discover a large medkit and a dose of steroids.

11 Blast the pods and collect the Shrinker ammo. Granting the chick's last request summons an Octabrain.

12 Proceed up the ramp quickly—the damaging blasts come from an indestructible fixture—and punish the initial resistance. Circling to the left allows you a shot at a cluster of gas canisters, which greatly evens the odds between you and the lurking load of Assault Commanders. Usually a couple will survive the detonation, but those can easily be shrunk to a manageable size. Checking the monitor will give you an idea how much fun you'll have while acquiring the blue key. Nearby, you can collect: two boxes of pipebombs, a Devastator, night vision goggles, and a red key.

13 En route to using the red key, be wary of unleashed Enforcers. On either side of the room that the ramp extends from, you should find a couple of boxes of ammo for the Devastator. You're about to use it up, big time.

14 Three hideous Boss Monsters protect the blue key. Baiting them to follow you outside is easily your best chance at victory. Draw them out, and then wait for them to emerge from around corners to get in your licks. With any luck at all, they'll follow one at a time. In the room is the godforsaken blue key, a large medkit, ammo for the chaingun, and the entrance to a secret place.

15 Secret place. As you stand looking at the control panel where you picked up the blue key, the monitor to the lower right will slide away to reveal this secret place. Inside are two trip-bombs and a Healing Atom.

16 Snuff the Enforcers. Checking the large room and the two small hallways nets RPG ammo and a portable medkit. Check the video monitor, throw the switch and check the monitor again. The door on the outer wall, near the overgrown area, is now open. If you have a jet pack, you can reach that area without throwing the switch from right where you're standing—but why waste the fuel?

17 Clear the hallways and control center of Enforcers. You'll also find Devastator ammo and a large medkit. When you're ready to rumble to the end of this mission, punch the switch near the opening that looks out onto the large room—but perhaps you could use a little tactical advice? Read on.

18 Have you had just about enough of these guys? I mean, do you get to take any ammo with you to the next mission? If you stand in the window and return fire, you are quite obviously dead. You're probably also running pretty damn low on ammo for both RPG and Devastator—what's a non-cheating Duke to do? Well, here's one thing you might try: Remember that these beasties have a genuine soft spot in their heads—if only there was some way you could take advantage of that without sucking in lead in harmful amounts.

Alright, alright, enough suspense.

Stand out of the beasts' line of sight. They have to see you to become agitated. Flip the switch and run downstairs. Don't let them see you.

Back on the floor of the room, kill the Enforcer that's recently arrived, and get out the pipebombs. The casing that surrounds the big bastards has sunken into the floor. If you move quickly to the extreme left and right of the structure, relatively right underneath each monster, you're not likely to attract attention. Toss 15 or 20 pipebombs at the extreme edges of the sunken casing, right up against the wall—again, right beneath the relative position of the guys up above. Head back upstairs quickly: You can't afford to let the monsters see you yet, or they'll start tossing grenades down on your head. With all the pipebombs in the vicinity...well, as Rainman might say: "Bad. Very bad."

Once you're back in the booth upstairs, dart across the window to let the monsters get a look. Once they've begun their attack, flip the switch on the wall once more. Wait about ten seconds, and emerge from hiding.

The scum are now re-encased in their big metal cocoon, with several pipebombs nestling their noggins. Detonating probably won't kill them outright, but it definitely takes the wind out of their scaly sails. Reopen the casing and you can probably finish them off with whatever ammo you have left. There's a large medkit on their landing. The button nearby unseals the room with the end-of-mission switch; but before you go inside, do test the Episode's first secret mission.

19 While standing on the large landing, facing the control booth, look high and to the right. Shoot that button, and a door opens on a secret place. The switch inside sends you to the secret mission, Spin Cycle. (Refer to the appendix for the walk-through).

MISSION 6: TIBERIUS STATION

If there's such a thing as a respite in Episode Two, this would be it. The Tiberius Station features plenty of goodies to gladden Duke's happy heart, and even a Boss Monster at the end of it all that can be entirely avoided if you play your cards right.

Be mindful not to pick up ammo and health unless you're really in need, and you can stock up pretty good at the Station. You'll need it for the missions ahead.

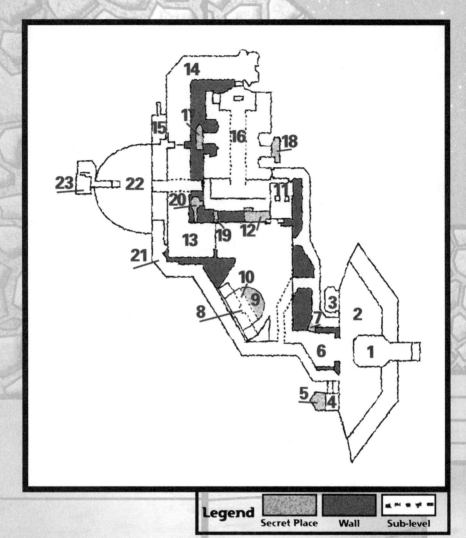

Legend		
Secret Place	Wall	Sub-level

HIGHLIGHTS

- Eight secret places
- Plenty of supplies
- A Boss Monster you can avoid entirely

MISSION 6: TIBERIUS STATION AT-A-GLANCE

1 Switches, pipebombs, pistol
2 Switches
3 Shotgun ammo, chaingun ammo, Shrinker and ammo, night vision goggles
4 Armor, medkit
* 5 Portable medkit
6 Switch
* 7 Shotgun ammo, Shrinker ammo
8 Water fountain
* 9 Pipebombs
10 Blue key, shotgun, pistol ammo, Holoduke, switches
11 Devastator, Healing Atom
*12 Chaingun ammo, steroids
13 Devastator ammo, medkit
14 RPG
15 Pistol ammo, chaingun ammo, laser tripbombs, medkit
16 Protective boots, medkit, switch, Freezethrower, scuba gear, medkit, shotgun ammo, night vision goggles, red key
*17 Healing Atoms
*18 RPG ammo
*19 Jet pack
*20 RPG
21 Freezethrower ammo, Shrinker ammo, portable medkit,
22 Chaingun
23 End

*Denotes secret place

Refueling at the Station

1   Blow the vent and hop into the Tiberius Station...a little too quiet, Dukeboy? After that last gauntlet, perhaps a breather is in order. Flip both switches—one turns on the lights, the other raises that big door—then collect the pipebombs and pistol and head downstairs.

2   Clean the large room of its Alien infestation. If you continue down the outside hallways, you'll come upon video monitors and switches. Each switch opens a door furthest from you in the big room. Tighten the laces on those Keds and cruise.

3   In the armory are two boxes of shotgun shells, two boxes of chaingun ammo, a Shrinker and additional ammo, and also a pair of night vision goggles. Load up.

4   Behind the door marked "Supplies" is just that: Two armor vests and a large medkit. There's also the entrance to a secret place.

5   Secret place. Open the wall between the two armor vests to reveal a room containing a portable medkit.

6   Entering the large, wide hallway, stop and throw the switch on your right to break off the gloom. The mirror at the end of the hall will make it seem that the advancing Aliens are coming from the left, but actually the hallway curves to the right. Once the welcome wagon has had its wheels knocked off, note the weak spot on the wall, above and to your right.

7   Secret place. Blowing open the wall reveals a secret place holding a box of shotgun shells. Exploring the accessible area of duct only nets another box of shells and some Shrinker ammo—and far too many Protozoid Slimers.

8   Blast the pods near the water fountain and rip the local Aliens a new one. Searching the wall across from the fountain pops you into a secret place.

9   Secret place. Here you'll find two boxes of pipebombs— yours for the taking, secretive Duke.

10 Upstairs, in the control booth, you'll discover the blue key, as well as a shotgun and some pistol ammo. Behind the unopened panel is yer old friend, Holoduke. The switch to the left of the window is for the lights, while the one to the right opens yonder door for a few seconds. Since you can't fit through the window, you have to dash for it. Put the elevator in the down position to speed your descent.

11 Kill the Enforcers and hail the Devastator. A Healing Atom rests in the niche above. Watch your step as you exit the room: A trio of Octabrain lurks in the hallway outside. Take care of business, then search the wall to the left of the door you just exited.

12 Secret place. Blast the Enforcer. In the wall panel is chaingun ammo and a dose of 'roids.

13 Approach the door with caution. Sentry Drones await on the other side; and once you enter the portal, a pair of laser tripbombs activate behind you. Hammer the Enforcers and keep one eye on that catwalk. Near the door where you entered is a box of ammo for the Devastator, and on the landing at the other end of the room is a large medkit. Note that you can jump on the top of the post outside this door and make a leap to the catwalk. Right now, it doesn't really benefit you to do so. But perhaps in Dukematch....

14 When you open this door, those gas canisters you see are reflected in a mirror at the end of the hall. Of course, it behooves you to blow them up—charge to the corner, pivot right and fire. That should thin out the crowd of Drones and Enforcers nearby. The wall blows open to reveal an RPG. Doubleback and relieve yourself before activating the blue key lock.

15 Through the door to the left of where you enter the hall are a pair of Aliens in various stages of inconvenience. Slay them in a most embarrassing fashion, and claim ammo for your pistol and chaingun, as well as a pair of laser tripbombs and a large medkit.

16 A pair of Duke boots lies to your right, and a large medkit can be found to your left as you enter the foyer. Octabrains and Enforcers await your emergence into the room proper. Throw the switch to build a bridge to the distant landing. Expect to attract more Octabrains when you bridge the gap,

and greet more Enforcers on the other side. All told, you can expect to acquire a Freezethrower, scuba gear, and a large medkit above the water, and shotgun ammo, night vision goggles, and the red key underwater. Note that the card looks yellow beneath the slime—take it topside, and it is, indeed, red.

> ## Tip!
> Be sure to enter the slimy deep in this room by utilizing the elevator near where you first entered; otherwise, getting back out requires a jet pack. Also, before you leave the room, be sure you've visited all three secret places.

17 Secret place. While swimming in the water, search the wall in the center alcove to the right as you enter the room. Inside the small chamber are two Healing Atoms.

18 Secret place. On the opposite side of the room, in the same relative location, is a similar secret place with two boxes of ammo for the RPG.

19 Secret place. Blowing open the puckered wall near the room's exit reveals a jet pack. Score!

> ## Tip!
> When you exit room (16), onto the previously sighted catwalk, be prepared to lob an RPG shell immediately, or you'll take serious damage from the turret at the other end of the bridge. Instead of crossing the bridge and using the key, however, look to your left and note the grate. There's a section of vent shaft you have yet to explore, and it's really in Duke's best interest to do a little vent crawling before ending this mission.

20 Secret place. That wooshing noise, as you cross through the lit area just inside the vent shaft, is a small door rising in the hallway, visible only when you exit the duct. Activate your jet pack ahead of time, and it's relatively easy to make it inside to claim the RPG cannon. As an amusing aside: That switch would serve well to seal this hiding place in Dukematch....

21 Explore the shaft and collect ammo for both the Freeze-thrower and the Shrinker, as well as a portable medkit. The grate to the left of the portable medkit leads to the Big Battle room of this mission, and if you enter from here you can clear out the riffraff without triggering the Boss Monster.

22 Kill the Octabrains and Slimers (and dispose of their pods). A chaingun lies on the floor.

At this point, you actually have the option of fighting the Boss Monster—another one of those big, armor-clad chain-gunning gorillas—or not. Should you choose not to face the BM, for whatever reason, it won't work against you when your body count is tabulated at the end of the mission.

To avoid the Costco size can of whupass, simply detonate the gas canisters and drop down into the resulting fissure. Near the location of the burning flame is an opening in the room's central column. Crawl inside and follow the tunnel, and you'll bypass the big bad guy and the locked door with the nuke sign on it. Inside the final room is a lone Enforcer. Should you wish to clean house in entirety, simply go outside and use that red key. Note that you have to actually step on the yellow and black striped line at the room's threshold to call the beast. If you hop over it, he won't show. Also, if you stand in front of the door and back up onto the bridge, the beast will arrive. Not until you do one of those two things does the brute come calling. You might take the opportunity to set a trap of some kind....

23 The door to the end-of-the-mission switch is locked from the inside. Crawl through the tunnel as previously described to reach the finish.

MISSION 7: LUNAR REACTOR

This mission is Nukem at its best: high body count, plenty of supplies, a slap on the face to Star Wars and a chance to put your pistol right up against the forehead of one of those behemoth Boss Monsters, free of charge. And what that'll do for your supply of Devastator ammo in the next mission is quite cool.

There's also another monstrous reactor to blow—the only thing missing is chicks, which is a little worrisome. Hopefully, that's because Duke's previous ass-kicking is putting a crimp in the Aliens' master plan.

Be aware that using a key in this mission not only opens up the obvious doorway, but also drops obstructions in the ductwork that can lead to increased effectiveness in dealing death.

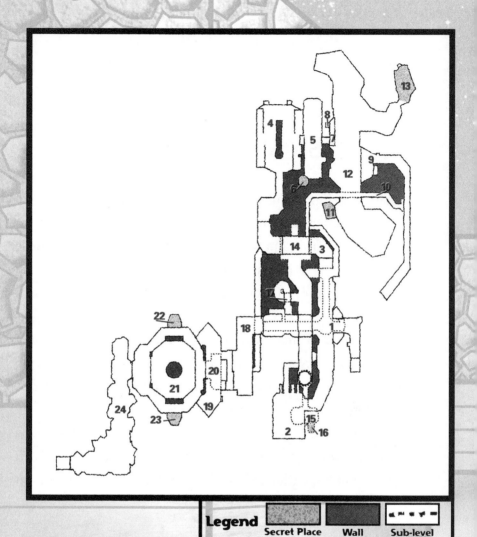

HIGHLIGHTS

- Seven secret places
- Plenty of Duke in a duct
- Boss Monster execution via pistol
- A special guest

Mission 7: Lunar Reactor At-a-Glance

1 Shotgun, night vision goggles, medkit, shotgun ammo, Devastator

2 Blue key, RPG, laser tripbomb, Devastator ammo, portable medkit, steroids

3 Blue key lock, Devastator ammo, medkit, shotgun ammo, Healing Atom

4 Chaingun cannon, pipebombs, Freezethrower ammo, armor, laser tripbomb, three medkits, chaingun ammo, medkit

5 Switches, medkit, shotgun ammo

* 6 Healing Atoms

7 RPG ammo

* 8 Chaingun ammo, medkit

9 Pistol ammo, yellow key, medkit

10 Shotgun ammo, medkit

*11 Armor, Healing Atom, RPG ammo

12 Jet pack

*13 Shrinker ammo, Shrinker

14 Night vision goggles, Freezethrower

15 Red key, medkits

*16 Freezethrower ammo, Holoduke

17 Medkit, protective boots, red key lock

18 Yellow key lock, Devastator ammo, pipebombs, chaingun ammo, laser tripbomb

19 Devastator ammo, night vision goggles, shotgun, laser tripbomb, medkit, water fountain

20 Shrinker ammo

21 Switch, medkit, shotgun ammo, RPG, Healing Atom

*22 Laser tripbombs, Devastator ammo

*23 RPG ammo

24 End

*Denotes secret place

MOON OVER MY AMMO

1   Perforate the Alien and check the monitor. As you enter, the panel to your left holds a shotgun and night vision goggles. Lob an RPG down to the end of the hallway as you round the corner to your left, and you'll dispose of a pair of Sentry Drones. There's more Aliens lurking in the central hallway, as well as a smattering (soon to be a splattering) of Protozoid Slimers. Cruising through the currently accessible area of ventilation shaft nets a large medkit, shotgun ammo, and a Devastator.

2   Check your looks and flush out the scumbags: Aliens and Enforcers. Cleaning the john garners a load of goodies: a blue key (in the flickering stall), an RPG, a laser tripbomb, Devastator ammo (one box lies on the floor, another through the floor-level grate behind a toilet), a portable medkit, and steroids.

3   Note that a trio of Enforcers seeks to prohibit the proper use of the blue key. Once you've illustrated your disdain for the vermin, open the door and RPG the Drone. Watch for Slimers and check the vent shaft above and to your right for more Devastator ammo. A large medkit is also in plain sight. At the end of this hallway is another of those Boss Monsters, eager to absorb some of that Devastator ammo you've been so judiciously hoarding. Before you make his acquaintance, you might blow out the grating at that end of the hallway and lob in an RPG—that'll help alleviate some of the Slimer problem. In that shaft is ammo for the shotgun, as well as a Healing Atom.

4   In the Crew Quarters proper awaits a hellacious firefight—more Aliens and Enforcers—but the payoff is sweet indeed. Use the hall to your advantage, drawing out the monsters a few at a time. Amidst the barracks you'll acquire a chaingun, pipebombs, and Freezethrower ammo. There's armor and a laser tripbomb in the lockers, and numerous small medkits scattered about. Check behind the panels on the wall for chaingun ammo and a large medkit.

5 Drop down the tunnel in the barracks. Throwing the switch will part the walls so that you can dash for the grating on the opposite side of the room, but notice the alcove to the right of the grating—you can also make a dash for that area, angling towards a large medkit and shotgun ammo therein. From that alcove, which also has a switch that parts the walls, it's a cakewalk to the next secret place. From the location of the switch, shoot out the grate before you make your move.

6 Secret place. Exit the alcove. To your left, the wall is flanked by a pair of large columns. The one on the right will slide upward to reveal a room with two Healing Atoms. Return and throw the switch in the previous alcove to continue.

7 An Alien patrols the landing you emerge on, but far more deadly is the laser turret mounted on the wall across the way. Polish off the three Aliens on the ledge opposite your position, pick up the box of RPG ammo, then search the walls for the opening to a secret place.

8 Secret place. Behind the console you'll find chaingun ammo and a large medkit, free of charge.

9 You can make it to the far ledge, without using the jet pack, with a tremendous leap. It's likely you'll take some damage, and certain you'll be greeted by a Slimer on the other side. Collect the pistol ammo; the yellow key sits in the niche just inside the entry to the hall. Proceed with extreme caution in the hallway—note its unstable nature, Dukeboy? When you step on the fissure about halfway down, all manner of hell breaks loose, as well as a good portion of the ceiling. Back far away, very quickly, and note the opening in the wall to your right. A large medkit lies just inside.

10 Making your way up the tunnel, expect Slimers and a pair of Aliens to snipe at you from the ledge where you first entered this canyon. When you've dealt with the Aliens, you can gain the top of the duct (blow a hole in it if the Aliens didn't) and spy a cave off to your left. Hello, secret place! Jumping in is no problem, but it's highly advisable to have at least a little jet pack fuel to get back out with—jumping back to the duct is a risky proposition. There's another pack on the canyon floor. Later on, when you're retracing your path and concluding this section of duct, you'll pick up more shotgun ammo and a large medkit.

11 Secret place. Inside the cave is armor, a Healing Atom and a box of ammo for the RPG. If you have any jet pack juice at all, now would be a good time to use it. Jump out of this cave and let yourself fall, then activate your jet pack at the last instant.

12 On the floor of the canyon is the aforementioned jet pack, and if you use it to cruise the canyon you'll discover the entrance to another secret place.

13 Secret place. There's Shrinker ammo in the front part of the cave, and a Shrinker in its entirety towards the back. There's also a Jedi Knight that someone has been treating kind of forcefully—expect a pair of Octabrain to feel lukewarm about your exploring—alright, we apologize for that one. If you're scrimping on fuel at this point, there is a teleporter hidden behind the wall near the dangling do-gooder. You'll arrive back on the ledge near where you found the yellow key.

14 Kick out the grate and get the attention of the local Octabrains. Any that don't come over to investigate can be pegged from the landing, where you'll also find a pair of night vision goggles. In plain sight from the ledge is a Freezethrower.

15 Ride down the scum rapids to the large gear, and let it carry you around to the left. Behind the cog is a short hallway and then a small room, guarded by two Enforcers. They protect the red key and two small medkits.

16 Secret place. One of the computer panels slides away to reveal another Enforcer, and he's all that stands between you, more Freezethrower ammo and a Holoduke.

17 Exiting the cog area, retrace your steps and climb the stairs across from the barrels. Kill the Octabrain near the large medkit (oh, the bitter irony that is Duke Nukem...). At the top of the stairs, an Alien defends a pair of protective boots and the red key lock, briefly. When you enter the area near the lock, you'll hear a familiar voice from your past. Using the red key also opens up some nearby duct area—providing increased access, but nothing more.

18 Entering the yellow key lock area, the Duke is greeted by two big, shiny new boxes of Devastator ammo. Now what could that be for? Perhaps they are for the two Boss Monsters to your left? Side by side, in this corridor, the two brutes presented an impressive logistical dilemma, even for the Dukebrain. There is a way to kill them, however—point blank and without taking a single drop of damage...with your pistol...interested?

Using the yellow key on the lock not only unlocks the big door, it also drops barriers in the nearby duct system. This allows you to enter through the vent on your right.

In order for this trick to work properly, first you have to rush through the big door and grab up the Devastator ammo, then rush back out before the door closes—as the monsters open fire. Now hop inside the vent shaft. Take a right and go to the end of that short section. Jump forward. Take another right, and proceed. One more right at the next intersection, and advance. You should be looking at the big "05" on the wall. Turn left. The passage slopes down, towards a box of pipebombs. The monsters are right outside the grate—on your right as you procure the bombs.

When you get the monsters' attention, some interesting things occur. Because of your proximity, they'll attack with their chainguns; but because of their orientation, they'll pour round after round into the wall below you, staring crazily into your eyes the whole time. One of them usually kills his buddy for you, shooting him in the back. Watch for bleeding, and move around if it doesn't seem the monsters are harming one another. Then simply take out your pistol and fire with impunity—point blank. Kind of like finding out how many licks it takes to get to the center of a Tootsie Pop....

Near the monitor is a box of ammo for the chaingun, and also a laser tripbomb. When you approach the monitor, an Enforcer attacks from the stairs.

19 Head upstairs first, clearing the stairway of an Enforcer and the large area itself of several Aliens. On the floor of the room you should find more Devastator ammo, night vision goggles, a shotgun, a laser tripbomb and a large medkit. There's also a water fountain for a thirsty Duke.

20 Downstairs are three more Enforcers, guarding a huge door, as well as ammo for the Shrinker.

21 Inside the large room is the heart of the reactor, plagued by a bad case of Enforcers, and perhaps a straggler Alien. In addition to the chaingun ammo you're bound to receive as a bonus for your homicidal tendencies, clean the walkway and control center of a large medkit, shotgun ammo, and an RPG cannon.

Time to use the clearly marked exit, Duke. First, you've got a reactor to blow.... The only problem is that when you do, an Assault Commander is going to come out of the door marked "EXIT," and he won't be pleased with your handiwork. A prudent Duke might lace the doorway with laser tripbombs—creating a deadly web for the big fat fly—before torching the evil machine.

The unique switch in the control area lowers the reactor's sheath, and any old RPG will bring the house down once the core is exposed. If you blast the device from one of the windows above, you'll be sure to avoid any harmful side-effects. Note that there is a Healing Atom inside the generator. Grab it after the deed is done, and you won't take damage from radiation bombardment. There's also two secret places, if you want to call them that....

22 Secret place. In the alcove above where you find the large medkit are a pair of laser tripbombs and ammo for the Devastator.

23 Secret place. In the alcove at the opposite end of the room is a box of ammo for the RPG.

24 The hallway leading to the final room is booby-trapped: A few steps down a series of nasty explosions rips the place apart. Run quickly back inside the reactor room when the fireworks start and you can avoid any personal damage. Three more Assault Commanders lie between you and the end-of-the-level switch.

MISSION 8: DARK SIDE

From a purely visual standpoint, this mission has some of the best Duking in the game. The Dark Side manages to be equal parts creepy and violent, and hey, what else do you want?

There's a special appearance by a miniature monolith a la *2001*, and also the button for the second secret mission in Episode Two: Lunatic Fringe. A single Boss Monster bars your way to the end of the mission, though a hoard of 20-odd Octabrain almost make up for the anti-climax.

Strap yourself in and get ready to rock. It's time to cast a little light on the Dark Side....

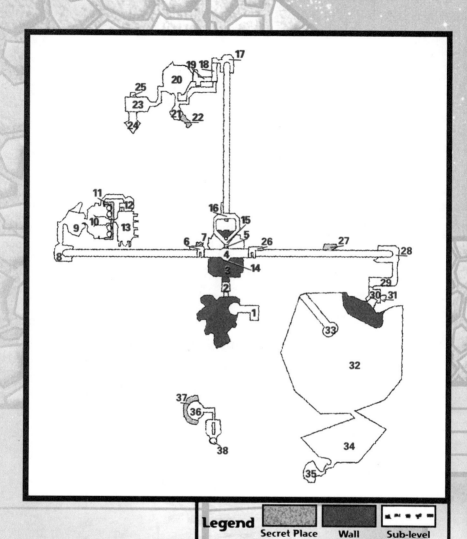

Legend

Secret Place	Wall	Sub-level

HIGHLIGHTS

- Seven secret places
- Speeding space trams
- The Monolith from *2001*, complete with soundtrack
- More than 200 enemies
- The entrance to a secret mission

Mission 8: Dark Side At-a-Glance

1 Pistol, medkit, armor
2 Shotgun
3 Medkit
4 Armor, Freezethrower, shotgun ammo, medkit
* 5 Healing Atoms
6 Pipebombs
* 7 Medkits, Devastator
8 Freezethrower ammo, medkit
9 Chaingun, medkit, Devastator ammo
10 Steroids, Shrinker ammo, portable medkit, two boxes of shotgun ammo, Holoduke, pipebombs, laser tripbomb
*11 Shrinker
12 Pipebombs, medkit
13 Blue key, chaingun ammo, armor, Healing Atom, RPG ammo, four medkits
14 Blue key lock, armor, night vision goggles
15 Medkits, Shrinker ammo, RPG, shotgun ammo
*16 Laser tripbombs, Shrinker
17 Devastator ammo, portable medkit
18 Healing Atom
19 Freezethrower ammo, shotgun ammo

20 Medkits, shotgun ammo
21 Shotgun
*22 Three boxes of pipebombs
23 RPG ammo, chaingun ammo, protective boots
24 Reactor
25 Yellow key, medkit, armor
26 Yellow key lock, medkit, pipebombs
*27 Healing Atoms
28 Devastator ammo, armor
29 Medkits
30 RPG ammo, Freezethrower ammo
31 RPG, shotgun ammo, medkit
32 RPG ammo, Devastator ammo, medkit
33 Devastator, medkit, Healing Atom
34 Pipebombs, medkit
35 Medkit, pipebombs
36 Pipebombs, Devastator ammo, Shrinker
*37 Secret mission entrance
38 Medkit, shotgun ammo, end

*Denotes secret place

Use of Force

1   Step into the Dark Side and bask in the glow. A pair of Enforcers are relaxing in the lunar gazebo, and it would be prudent to deal with them and the nearby Slimer pods before scooping up the pistol and large medkit. There's also an armor vest nearby. The courtyard outside is vacant and inaccessible.

2   Cause a pair of Aliens to perish shortly after you exit the elevator. Grab the shotgun, if you need it.

3   Expect a mad rush when you open the door: the chaingun works nicely to slaughter the Aliens and Enforcer while keeping the Sentry Drones at bay. A large medkit awaits near the door.

4   More Enforcers patrol the halls to your right and left in the central hub. Take them out, pick up any items you need, and search for the secret place.

5   Secret place. The schematic diagram that you face as you enter the hub slides away to reveal a pair of Healing Atoms.

6   Through the door marked "Alpha Transport," two more Aliens prepare to meet their maker. On the ground nearby is a box of pipebombs, and if you use one on the weak wall, across from the switch, you'll discover another secret place.

7   Secret place. An Alien and a pod try vainly to keep you from two small medkits and the Devastator.

8   When you throw the switch on the wall, a tram arrives carrying three Aliens. From the secret place, it's quite satisfying to let an RPG rattle around in their car. At the end of the line, more Aliens await, as does a large medkit and ammo for the Freezethrower.

9   Tripping the laser bombs in this room invites Enforcers to attack from behind, in addition to the ones waiting in plain sight. When you set foot in the room, an earthquake reveals a cavern filled with pods to your left. In the cavern rests a chaingun, near a large medkit. You'll find a box of ammo for the Devastator in what remains of the room itself.

10 Clean out the Aliens, and reap the benefits: 'roids, Shrinker ammo, a portable medkit, two boxes of shotgun ammo, a Holoduke, pipebombs, and a laser tripbomb. Begin searching for the secret place.

11 Secret place. As you stand facing the liquid-filled tanks in the previous room, turn to your left or right, depending on which wing you occupy. That large column slides upward to reveal a small chamber with an elevator, leading to a connecting hallway full of Aliens and pods. You can drop down inside the tanks from here—netting a Shrinker and also releasing more Aliens in the room outside.

12 Hop on the conveyor belt and make your way through the obstacles to a room guarded by Octabrains. Most of them are below the water, and the one that greets you from the landing will submerge as well if given the chance.... If ever there was a time for the ol' Holoduke-and-pipebomb fishing trick, this be it. Beneath the slime you'll find another box of pipebombs and a small medkit.

13 Ride the elevator up from the slime pit and kill the Alien. For sheer destructive pleasure, place pipebombs near the ground-level wall nooks and tripbomb the other doorway: when you make a grab for the goodies, Slimers and Aliens pour into the room to punish you—not today, vermin. Trying to get pipebombs to stay in the upper nooks isn't really worth the effort, so do have that shotgun handy when acquiring the blue key and the chaingun ammo. In the upper nooks you'll discover armor, a Healing Atom and ammo for the RPG. There are also three small medkits nearby. Upstairs, dispose of the newly arrived Enforcers on your way to the blue key lock.

14 A door in the wall opens to your left when you access the blue key lock. Ride the elevator up and dispatch the trio of Aliens. Armor, a large medkit and night vision goggles lie nearby.

15 Between you and the Gamma Transport lurks a horde of Enforcers. Before boarding the train, check the newly accessible region for various items and the entrance to a secret place—look behind the schematic on the wall near the transport.

16 Secret place. Here you'll discover a pair of laser tripbombs and a Shrinker.

17 Hammer the Enforcers awaiting your arrival. A box of ammo for the Devastator lies nearby, and behind the wall panel is another portable medkit.

18 Descend the elevator after pipepbombing the area below. Rid the vent shaft of an Alien and several Slimers to collect a Healing Atom. Double back to the door when you reach the slime flow—tactically, it's to your advantage to enter this area through the front door.

19 When you enter the long hallway, explosions open two gaping holes in the walls and release a herd of Enforcers. You can stay and slug it out, or retreat to the top of the elevator behind you for more pipebomb fun. In the exploded areas of the hallway, you'll discover ammo for both the Freezethrower and shotgun.

20 Be prepared for a Drone rush when you open the door. A well placed RPG shot, slightly above and to your left as you face the door, can catch most of them in an alcove across the room. Enforcers patrol the walkway on both sides of the pit, which is brimming with Octabrains. Along the walkway you'll discover a large medkit, two small medkits and shotgun ammo. Once you've collected the goodies, backtrack to the vent once more. There's also some chicks in need of mercy.

21 Back in the vent, it's pretty easy to bait the remaining Octabrains into your sights—just give them a peek at you or whip out ol' Holoduke. Grant last requests and pick up the shotgun, then blast the weak spot in the wall to reveal a secret place.

22 Secret place. Three (count 'em; three) boxes of pipebombs. Hopefully that'll help the mood of a troubled Duke.

23 Assault Commanders and Enforcers await a rapid demise. Oblige them and check the floor of the room for RPG ammo, chaingun ammo, protective booties, and a ledge you can't quite reach.

24 Open the large double doors by standing off to one side, or you'll take damage from the reactor in this room. Toss in a

pipebomb, close the doors back up again, and back way off. The resultant explosion rips up the floor, providing a ramp up to the ledge.

25 On the ledge is the yellow key, a large medkit and also some armor. Be ready for the Enforcer posse that arrives when you start poking around: They come through the door where you first entered.

26 Accessing the yellow key lock gives entry to the Beta Station, guarded by Enforcers for a short time. Be mindful of the one hanging in the duct above the area of the schematic and the monitor. You'll want him cleaned out of there: That duct is where you'll arrive when you teleport from the nearby secret place. Also nearby, you'll discover a large medkit and pipebombs.

27 Secret place. As the train shoots through the tunnel, press up against the wall, through the car's open doorway. About halfway down the tunnel, you'll pop into a room with an Alien, a pair of Healing Atoms, and a teleporter. The teleporter (a one-way job) pops you back to the station you just left. Recall the car and ride on, Dukeman.

28 Kill the Alien scum waiting for the train and disembark; nearby is Devastator ammo and behind the sliding panel is an armor vest.

29 Enforcers and a Sentry Drone try to soften you up before the end of the mission. Punish them, and scoop up the two small medkits on the floor nearby.

30 Adjust the attitude of the local Alien population and collect ammo for RPG and Freezethrower.

31 Amidst the spacesuits you'll find an RPG, shotgun ammo, and a large medkit.

32 In the huge lunar arena you'll be greeted by a nasty swarm of Sentry Drones, pouring from the underside of the huge construction. Try RPG fire initially—they display a disturbing tendency to dodge Devastator fire—and then switch to the chaingun. You can also try retreating to the previous room and filling the decompression chamber with a few pipebombs—luring them to their doom. Once you clear the

arena of the few stragglers, check the surrounding area for RPG ammo, Devastator ammo and a large medkit.

33 Inside the huge arm-like structure are Enforcers and Aliens, as well as a Devastator and a large medkit. Throw the switch on the wall to reveal a Health Atom, and also drop the force-field on the big ape outside. If you'd like to make a grand entrance for the battle, go ahead and drop through the hole in the floor.

34 Expect resistance from Drones and Enforcers as you explore the canyon. You'll also discover a box of pipebombs and a large medkit, right about the time you're ambushed by a pair of Assault Commanders. In the cave where the floating freaks were co-habitating is a weak wall. Blow it.

35 Holy *2001*, Dukeman! Alien scum making a mockery of monolithic proportions need to be taught some manners. Grab the large medkit and the box of pipebombs, then heed the scrawled advice: Plunging into the black slab teleports you to still weirder places, and you might try sending some ammo along ahead of you to soften the arrival.

36 When you exit the slab, run into the hallway directly in front of you, then turn and engage. Kill the Octabrains and splat-ter the pods. Collect pipebombs, ammo for the Devastator, and a Shrinker. As you stand facing the monolith, from just outside the hallway, look to your right and high on the wall, above that edge of the slime trough. Hopefully, Dukeboy, by now you know what to do with the weak spot on the wall.

37 Secret place. Inside this secret place is a big secret indeed—the trigger that transports you to a secret mission: Lunatic Fringe. Whatever you do, Duke, save your game before you venture to the Fringe. It's basically a huge arena filled with monsters and ammo, and whether or not you make it out with a net gain is more luck than skill. If you go there, you'll begin the final mission when you leave. Our advice: Finish this level—do everything but hit the switch—then come back and save the game to another slot before you plunge into the Fringe. You'll be damn glad you did. (Refer to Appendix A for more information on Lunatic Fringe.)

38 A serious bunch of Octabrains bars your entrance to the end-of-the-level switch, but it's relatively easy to bait them into RPG range by backing into the hallway. On the ground

nearby is a large medkit, as well as two boxes of ammo for the shotgun. Granting sweet release to the damsels in distress ushers in another herd of Octabrain. Try lacing the area with pipebombs unless you want to deal with each individually. The end-of-the-level switch is located beneath the water.

MISSION 9: OVERLORD

The Overlord of the moon awaits our hero—and Duke has a fitting demise in mind for the hulking freak from another world.

This mission is actually relatively tame by Duke standards, at least as far as the actual combat goes. The ending sequence...well, if you don't know, we don't want to spoil it.

Hang onto your Devastator ammo, and use the RPG sparingly. You'll need all of it to take down the big bozo and finish this little episode in the life of Duke Nukem.

Also, be mindful of time spent underwater; there's a few scuba tanks lying about, but not enough to get careless. You have a lot of Duke dunking to do, as evidenced by the fact that this mission starts underwater.

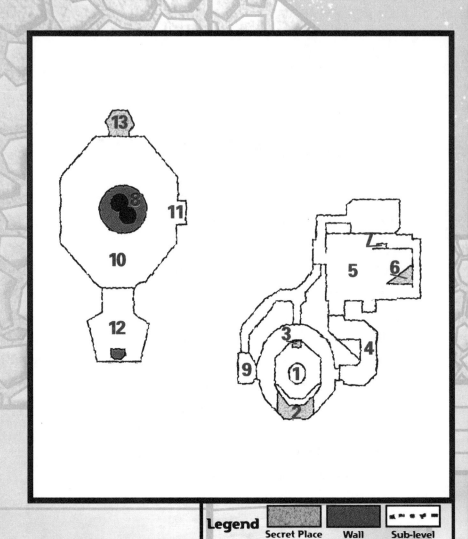

HIGHLIGHTS

- Four secret places
- Gratuitous head-ripping
- Intestinal voiding

MISSION 9: OVERLORD AT-A-GLANCE

1 Pistol, scuba gear, shotgun ammo, Freezethrower, button puzzle (****). Beneath the water: shotgun, medkit, Freezethrower ammo, switch, Healing Atom, shotgun ammo

* 2 Armor, Freezethrower ammo, Healing Atom

* 3 RPG

4 Medkits, Devastator ammo, shotgun ammo, portable medkit

5 Shrinker, RPG ammo, armor, medkit, scuba gear, Freezethrower ammo, RPG, night vision goggles, Shrinker ammo, switch. Underwater: medkit, Holoduke

* 6 Pipebomb

7 Healing Atom

8 Healing Atom, pipebombs

9 Armor, small medkit, night vision goggles, chaingun

10 Large medkits, laser tripbombs, Devastator ammo

11 Jet pack, Devastator, portable medkit

12 Four boxes RPG ammo, Healing Atom, end

*13 RPG ammo, portable medkit, Healing Atom, Devastator ammo

*Denotes secret place

THE THRILL OF VICTORY

1 Swim through the tunnel and surface quickly—the Octabrains can wait. Kill the Aliens and Enforcers, and search the perimeter of the room for a pistol, scuba gear, and shotgun ammo. To lower the central column and claim the Freezethrower, the button puzzle combo is: **. Beneath the water you'll find a shotgun, a large medkit, and ammo for the Freezethrower. Pressing the handprint on the wall opens a panel in the central column to reveal a Healing Atom, and there's another box of shotgun ammo within reach; down the tunnel before a forcefield bars your way.

2 Secret place. From the pool, search the walls on either side of the control center window. In you'll pop to a place with armor, Freezethrower ammo and a Healing Atom.

3 Secret place. After lowering the central column, a panel will open when you jump on to claim the Freezethrower. The panel is on the other side of the column nearest the duct grating, and inside the room is an RPG.

4 Open the door and proceed with caution: A Boss Monster waits just around the bend. There's a small medkit nearby, as well as ammo for the Devastator. Behind the picture of the planet on the wall is a compartment containing a large medkit and two boxes of shotgun shells. If the firefight with the big ape doesn't blow open the weak wall, utilize the canisters nearby to reveal a portable medkit.

5 Move quickly as you enter this room, which is crawling with Enforcers, Aliens, and Protozoid Slimers. Take a right, hop the waterway and enter the hall. Pause and take out any pursuit before you continue. At the top of the stairs are more Enforcers, and once they've been reduced to body parts you can snipe quite effectively at a gang of Aliens from that position.

   The landing nearby needs to have a serious pod problem solved. Once that's done, you can gather up a Shrinker and ammo for the RPG. Killing the chick reveals an armor vest, as well as ushering in an Octabrain.

   Jump to the platform across the way and continue pummeling pods. Usually, this gets the attention of more Enforcers and an Alien. A large medkit lies nearby, and blasting the babe calls in another big-headed bastard. Behind the cocoon is another set of aqua gear.

Ammo for the Freezethrower sits on the stairway leading up, almost distracting you from the descending Octabrain. Upstairs are more pods and a bevy of dangling beauties. An RPG awaits your approval, and there's also night vision goggles, and Shrinker ammo nearby.

Once you granted last requests and welcomed the arriving Octabrains in the only proper manner, throw the switch on the wall. It drops a forcefield in a nearby duct, which is where you're headed next. Right after you clear the area underwater of more Octabrains, which are defending a large medkit and Holoduke. Note that down that tunnel, a switch on the wall drops the forcefield you first encountered from the other side.

Check the duct, at the bottom of the stairs from where the Freezethrower lay, right after you investigate the two nearby secret places.

6   Secret place. The wall of the first hallway you entered in room (5) just needs a little nudge—about an RPGs worth—to give way on the left. Inside is a secret place, loaded with two boxes of pipebombs.

7   Secret place. From the first landing in room (3), hug the wall on your right as you approach the waterfall: in you pop to a secret place, acquiring a Healing Atom.

8   At the end of the shaft you're looking into an area with a large, spinning blade, soon to be teaming with Octabrains. Perhaps you should let Holoduke make the initial introductions.... When the coast is clear, hop down onto the blade and collect the Healing Atom. From there, you'll discover two boxes of pipebombs (in the shaft leading to the first room of this mission).

9   The other avenue contains Enforcers, and leads to a room full of Aliens and bountiful booty: armor, a small medkit, night vision goggles, and a chaingun. This room also opens onto the mission's first encounter area, via the handlock at doorside. Return to the area with the huge blade, and drop down the shaft.

10 At the bottom of the large duct is a pod hatchery of grim proportions. Fortunately, those canisters laced throughout are ripe for providing destruction on a scale that is most

satisfying. Strafe with the chaingun to the right of the big door, and enjoy. First of all: Don't go near the large door until you're ready for it to open. Inside is the end-of-the-Episode badass. Avoid that large medkit for now; there's another nearby, as well as a pair of laser tripbombs and two boxes of ammo for the Devastator. Visit the next area to complete your stockpiling before summoning the Lord Scum.

11 Hop through the hole in the wall and submerge thyself. Below, Octabrain guard a jet pack, a Devastator, and a portable medkit. Ready to rock?

12 The big bad guy is plenty big, and he packs quite a wallop, but a mobile Duke won't have much to fear. A full compliment of Devastator ammo will easily do the trick, and if you get in a bind, you can run into the room the Alien comes out of. Close the door behind you (there's a switch just inside) and grab a refill: four boxes of RPG ammo and a Healing Atom. Ah, the relief of victory....

13 Secret place. Should you still be in need of sustenance, when you exit the Big Boss' room, notice there's a hole in the wall across from you. Inside awaits two boxes of RPG ammo, a portable medkit, a Healing Atom and ammo for the Devastator.

CHAPTER 6
EPISODE THREE
SHRAPNEL CITY

The Man is back in town for Episode Three.

Having hammered a horde of lunar losers, there now remains only the final confrontation on Mother Earth.

The third *Duke Nukem* episode features no new gadgets but still boasts plenty of surprises, as our hero's journey takes him through flood zones and subways, enduring an earthquake and another bad trip for the Duke ride.

For the most part, the missions ahead are smaller than those that have come before, at least in the spatial sense. The traps are more deadly, with waves of villains in close confines, so there's still plenty of combat...but there's less to explore once the monsters have been removed, which is a bit of a disappointment.

Points of contention aside, this episode features some of the best missions in the whole game. The gems here really shine, and so the others become almost welcome respites from the fray.

At the end of it all lies the final showdown, with the fate of the planet—and every last chick—hanging in the balance. Slap in that clip and head for the city, Nukem. It's time to take care of those alien bastards once and for all.

MISSION 1: RAW MEAT

The first mission of Episode Three returns Duke to good old terra firma, with a vengeance. Surviving the first few encounters of Raw Meat is the trick—once you get past the initial confrontations, things become a little less frantic.

For those of you playing the game through sequentially, this mission marks the return of the Pig Cop to Duke's crosshairs, as the game designers saw fit to deprive us of any "Pigs in Space" references throughout Lunar Apocalypse.

Duke's patience is running low, and like Rowdy Roddy Piper (*They Live*; check it out) he's all out of bubble gum.

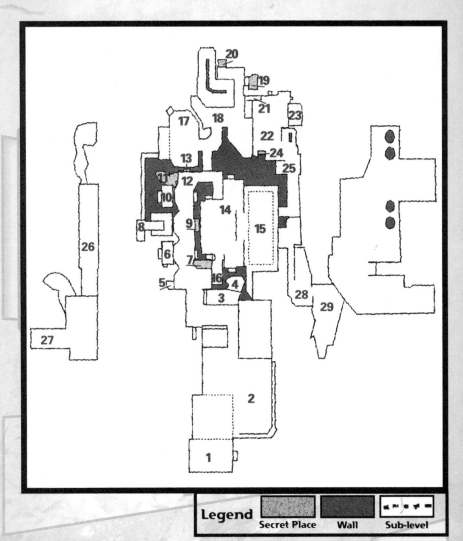

Legend	Secret Place	Wall	Sub-level

HIGHLIGHTS

- Seven secret areas
- Duke Nukem karaoke
- Pig Cops aplenty

MISSION 1: RAW MEAT AT A GLANCE

1 Devastator

2 Healing Atom, chaingun cannon

3 Pipebombs, Healing Atom

4 Chaingun ammo, medkit

5 Shotgun ammo, medkit

6 Shotgun, jet pack

* **7** Chaingun ammo, medkit

8 Steroids, switch

* **9** Shrinker

10 Portable medkit

* **11** Shrinker ammo, medkit

12 Night vision goggles

* **13** Armor

14 Shotgun ammo, medkit, chaingun ammo

15 Scuba gear

16 Blue key, medkit, switches

17 Blue key lock, shotgun ammo, RPG

18 Steroids, Devastator ammo, Shrinker ammo, Healing Atom, pipebomb

19 Night vision goggles, pipebombs, chaingun ammo

* **20** Freezethrower

21 Laser tripbomb

22 Medkit, jet pack, Armor, Healing Atom

23 Shotgun ammo, Freezethrower ammo, medkit

* **24** RPG ammo

25 Red key lock

26 Ammo for chaingun, shotgun, Devastator, red key

27 Chaingun ammo, pipebombs, Holoduke, medkit

28 Exploding wall

29 Medkit, End

*Denotes secret place

Duke Ain't for Dinner

1 As Episode Three begins, you have to make some quick decisions to gain the courtyard below and still have a fighting chance in the mission ahead. Grab the Devastator out of the wall panel to your right, then move towards the left of the roof. That'll draw an Enforcer to his death, and if you're lucky he'll drop a chaingun. If not, at least repeat the process until he spits up ammo: the chaingun is nearby.

   Next, move to the right corner of the roof. Kill any Aliens you can from that vantage point, and be mindful of Drones nearby. There are two, and one will be patrolling just beneath you. Try not to land on top of him when you jump—a running leap serves nicely. Sometimes you can bait the drones up to rooftop level.

2 When you hit the courtyard, defend yourself against the Aliens and Drones with gusto. The incline gives access to the building's ledge nearby, where you'll find a Healing Atom and the chaingun cannon, as well as attracting more attention from Aliens.

3 Make your way up the ramp flanked by the white partitions, slaughtering the Enforcers and quickly taking out the wall-mounted laser turret, which targets you as you gain the first landing. As you approach the top of the second landing, hop over the white wall on your right and discover a box of pipebombs, a Healing Atom, and a weak spot in the wall....

4 Blowing the wall reveals a small pool of water. Under the surface are a surly assortment of sharks and Octabrains, but you can quickly grab a nearby load of chaingun ammo, and perhaps the small medkit, then surface back in the courtyard outside. Dispose of the Aliens that greet you and continue on up the ramp.

5 As you enter the building, blast the turret at the far end of the hall. Look to your left and note the green wall. When you approach the "Dukai Sushi" sign, that wall slides away to unleash a drone, and a near by turret activates. If you lay a pipebomb in front of the wall, and back quickly outside after tripping the trap, you'll at least take care of the turret. Inside the nook are shotgun shells and a small medkit.

6   The door to the first room on your left slides open as you advance. Inside are four Aliens dining on shotgun. A panel in the wall slides aside to reveal the jet pack.

7   Secret Place. To enter the area behind the "Dukai Sushi" sign, stand facing the wall around the corner to the left of the sign. Jump up and forward, and you'll discover a narrow area with chaingun ammo and a small medkit. Other areas are accessible from here, but we know what a stickler for orderly procedures you are...trust us, and return to the large hallway.

8   Entering the second room, the table sinks into the floor to reveal a short tunnel. In the room beyond are steroids and a monitor. Get a preview, and throw the switch to open a door up ahead of you.

9   Secret Place. Across from the previous room, the "Exotica Tonight" billboard sinks when searched to reveal the Shrinker.

10 Grab the portable medkit off the table, prepared for the two Aliens who rush you from behind shortly thereafter. There's also a weak spot in the wall in need of that special Duke touch.

11 Secret Place. A stash of Shrinker ammo and two large medkits await, but beware. If you try to take the Shrinker ammo, and the fire damages you, you'll suck down those two medkits the instant your health dips below 100.

12 In this nook are the night vision goggles, and using them reveals an invitation to debauchery. Now who could the message refer to? Bad Duke. Naughty Duke. Bad.

13 Secret Place. Behind the menu on the wall is a secret place, and an Armor vest to call your own.

14 Down the hallway, the door is open thanks to your earlier switch-throwing. Detonate the canisters to start the cleaning process, and be ready for the Alien that teleports in near your right shoulder. Once all the Aliens have been dispatched, you can collect shotgun ammo, a small medkit, and chaingun ammo from the tables nearby. Each time you make a grab, expect Octabrain attacks.

15 Shoot the Enforcer through the large window, then jet pack over and grab the scuba gear. A card key is below the water, but by the time you need it you'll find a much better avenue of approach.

16 Blast the Enforcers and claim the blue key and small medkit. The switch opens the door connecting the front lobby, and activating the cash register reveals a network of teleporters throughout the lobby and the room you just came through. Not real useful right now, but during a Dukematch....

17 Activating the blue key lock grants access to the bar, which would really be far more appealing if the walls were splattered with Pig Cop blood.... When you've finished redecorating, gather up shotgun ammo and the RPG (from behind the speaker). Climbing on-stage triggers the arrival of more Pig Cops and an Enforcer, and blasting the babe invites Aliens. Note that it's possible to jump through the "Exotica Tonight" poster, and teleport back to the front of the building. You can also use the jet pack to explore the short, empty expanse of ventilation duct.

Tip!

Step up to the microphone for a little karaoke Duke. At least they're playing your song...don't quit your day job.

---

18 Regardless of the presentation, Pig Cop slop leaves a little to be desired. Floating amid the debris, scarf up steroids, ammo for the Devastator, Shrinker ammo, a Healing Atom, and a stray pipebomb.

19 Checking the low cupboard near the vent shaft reveals night vision goggles, and pushing the wall inside opens a room containing pipebombs and ammo for the chaingun cannon.

20 Secret Place. When you exit the cupboard, press the hand print on the wall to reveal a nearby room holding a Freezer.

21 Blow open the vent shaft in room (19) and hop inside to discover a laser tripbomb. Blow the fan at the other end, and soften up the crowd in the next room with a couple

of pipebombs. Then double back and go through the front door.

22 Clear out the remaining Aliens and Enforcers. Behind the clearly marked panel is a large medkit, and a small portion of the wall slides away above the grill to reveal another jet pack. There's also Armor in a nook behind the door where you entered, and a Healing Atom near the tub of water.

23 Entering the large refrigerator invites more Aliens and an Enforcer, but nets you ammo for both shotgun and Freezethrower, as well as a large medkit.

24 Secret Place. The wine racks slide to reveal a welcome sight—two boxes of ammo for the RPG.

25 Pig Cops guard the area near the red key lock, and if you drop down inside that tub of water in the previous area, you'll wage a battle royale for the red card key.

26 Octabrains and pods attempt to keep you from the merciful release of chicks, as well as ammo for the chaingun, shotgun, and Devastator, and the red key.

27 Deflate the Octabrains and smash the pods. Collect ammo for the chaingun, some pipebombs, Holoduke, and even a small medkit. The most expedient way to leave this area is probably through the fissure you opened near the beginning of this mission. There are four Aliens waiting topside, and they are ripe for extermination if you coax them to land in that narrow alley.

28 Use the red key and pop open the garage door, just to be thorough. In the area up the ramp are two Enforcers, and as you crest the rise, explosions to your left open up the final room of this mission.

29 Kill the Aliens hiding on the other side of the flames and claim one last large medkit. The end-of-the-level switch is nearby.

MISSION 2: BANK ROLL

Those Alien maggots are crawling all over a Federal office in the Bank Roll mission, and it's up to Duke to make sure they pay a substantial penalty.

Episode Three begins to pick up steam here, as the One Who Nukes wades through a riotous roll call of Pig Cops, Octabrain, and Aliens. Kind of like old home week on the Duke farm, with a couple of Boss Monsters thrown in at the end for good measure. 'Nuff said.

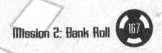

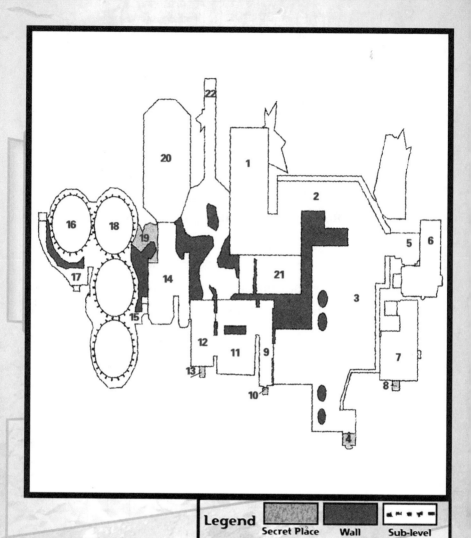

Legend   Secret Place   Wall   Sub-level

HIGHLIGHTS

- Five secret areas
- Vault full of monsters
- One HUGE explosion

Mission 2: Bank Roll At a Glance

1 Pipebombs, shotgun, shotgun ammo, steroids, portable medkit

2 Medkit, pistol

3 Medkit, pipebombs, ammo for Devastator and Freezethrower, Armor, laser tripbombs, Healing Atom

* 4 Chaingun cannon

5 Pipebombs

6 Freezethrower, Healing Atom, chaingun ammo, drinking fountain

7 Ammo for RPG and Freezethrower, steroids, button, blue key

* 8 Devastator

9 Blue key lock, medkit, button

*10 Holoduke

11 Laser tripbomb, medkit, Shrinker ammo, shotgun ammo

12 Medkit, button

*13 Medkits, jet pack

14 Medkit, Shrinker

15 Protective boots

16 Medkit, switch

17 Red key, boots, jet pack

18 Weak spot on wall

*19 Healing Atom

20 Vault

21 Shotgun ammo, RPG

22 Portable medkit, End

*Denotes secret place

No Deposit, No Return

1   Dispatch the Pig Cops and Enforcer across the way, and check the area where you arrive for a box of pipebombs. There's also a shotgun and some shells nearby. Destroying the cluster of trashcans yields a fresh supply of steroids, and a Slimer to slay. Dumpster diving reveals a portable medkit, and also brings a Pig Cop runnin'.

2   An Enforcer guards a large medkit, and calls for back-up when you make the grab for his stash. There's also a Pig Cop lurking nearby, ready to part with a pistol.

3   Pig Cops, one in a patrol vehicle, along with Aliens and Enforcers inhabit the area in front of the Federal Loan and Trust. Once they've been paid off, with interest, search nearby for a large medkit, more pipebombs, and ammo for both Devastator and Freezethrower. Be Ready—when you explore the nook near the Devastator ammo, an Assault Commander appears in the courtyard outside. Perhaps he was nervous about you finding his secret place.... PS: don't forget to climb onto the building's ledge for Armor, two laser tripbombs, and a Healing Atom.

4   Secret Place. Either ATM machine slides up to reveal a small room with a chaingun cannon inside.

5   As you approach this door, all manner of hell, and quite a few Pig Cops, break loose. Through the garage door in front of you comes a recon vehicle and swine, while the window on your right opens to issue forth more foul foes. Dispense justice, and grab the pipebombs on the ground nearby.

6   A Freezethrower, Healing Atom, and chaingun ammo await inside, and there's even a drinking fountain you might want to hit before getting automatically healthy. Hop the elevator.

7   Upstairs, a small gang of Enforcers need to be told it's quittin' time. Once they've been properly punched out, along with the Pig Cop cringing in the cubicle, gather up ammo for the RPG and Freezer, and still more 'roids. Push the button on the front of the desk to lower the bookcase, and reveal the blue key. At the same time, a nearby secret place is revealed.

8   Secret Place. Pushing the button on the desk slides aside the large picture, revealing a Devastator weapon.

9   Access the blue key lock and enter the Loan and Trust. Slay the Pig Cop cowering in the shadows to your right. A large medkit lies nearby, and above where the Pig Cop perished is a button on the wall. Shooting it reveals a secret place.

10 Secret Place. Shoot the button and the phones rise to reveal a small compartment and the Holoduke himself.

11 Pig Cops and Enforcers crowd the lobby and jostle for position behind the counter. Try to take care of them from a distance, as well as the turrets overhead. A laser tripbomb trap activates across the doorway once you venture into the room. A large medkit and ammo for the Shrinker adorn the lobby, and a box of shotgun shells sits in the teller's window.

12 Two sneakin' Pig Cops attempt to perforate your manly backside when you cross behind the counter. Look on the floor for a small medkit, and push the button on the desk to unlock the large door. Don't leave without opening the nearby secret place.

13 Secret Place. The picture on the wall slides away to reveal a niche containing two small medkits and a jet pack.

14 Slay the Enforcers and study the vault. A large medkit sits nearby, and a Shrinker lies between the switch and the wall panel. Push all three switches on the desk to access the next room through the small door.

15 Jump on the dais and grab the protective boots—you're going to need them. From that pedestal, turn and look to your left, through the slit now visible in the gears. Go jump on the dais in that room.
    At this point, the gigantic gears are actually aligned like you need them to be. Don't put yourself up on any more pedestals, so to speak, and you're in business.

16 Make your way to the center of the Delta gear—a large medkit is on the floor—and get ready to run. When you hop on the Delta pedestal, watch the large opening track across the edge of the room, and a doorway becomes visible. Run through that door, and throw the switch on the wall to the "open" position.

17 Ride the elevator up and kill the Pig Cops and Enforcer. The red key sits on the floor, waiting for someone Duke enough to use it. The button on the wall opens a panel with another pair of boots and a jet pack.

18 From the previous room, jump out the doorway and into the center of the Gamma cog. Jump up on the pedestal, and the gear rotates to reveal a weak spot in the wall. Stand back, and let 'er rip to reveal a secret place.

19 Secret Place. A serious shortcut, as well as a Healing Atom, stands revealed when you blast the wall.

20 Inside the vault are a pair of Boss Monsters and a major Octabrain convention. As soon as you open the vault door, retreat back to the office area, dropping Holoduke so that he attracts the Octas, and so you can snipe at them from the other doorway. Peek inside the vault: note the canisters. Blowing them opens up walls throughout this level—an area crawling with Octabrain.

   After the tremendous explosion, one of the Boss Monsters may try to hide in a nook to the right of the door as you look into the vault. If you step to the left of the door, the current carries you slowly in his direction. Devastate the big space monkey. The other one is sure to be somewhere nearby, and both are probably still smarting from the vault explosion. Show them how much you care.

21 After clearing the Octabrains, you have a chance to search the area where the Pig Cops were shooting from when the mission began. Those two rooms yield shotgun ammo and an RPG cannon.

22 Near the end-of-the-level switch is a portable medkit. Yer outta here, Dukeboy.

MISSION 3: FLOOD ZONE

Scuba Duba Duke time in the Flood Zone, easily one of the best of all the Nukem missions. This baby has it all, and with a good chunk of the melee under water, you have to be quick as well as deadly.

Which brings up an important point: watch how you use that scuba tank. There's one at the very beginning of the mission, and another toward the end. If you bring any with you as the mission begins, use it up first, then jet pack back for the obvious refill. The second one is in a secret place, requiring you to trip a nasty trap to gain access. You can really get it at any time, so if you get in a pinch, read ahead to see how it's revealed.

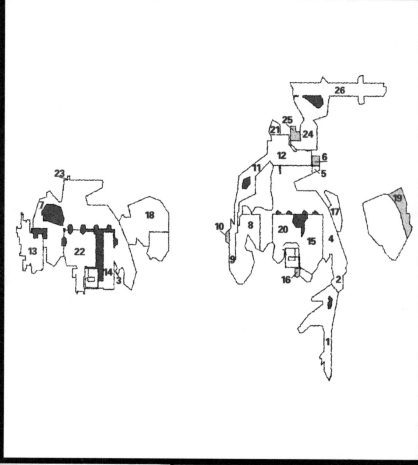

Legend
Secret Place   Wall   Sub-level

HIGHLIGHTS

- Five secret areas
- Serious underwater combat
- Tricky traps and sneaky secrets

MISSION 3: FLOOD ZONE AT A GLANCE

  1 Scuba tank, medkit, RPG, shotgun ammo

  2 Medkit, pistol

  3 RPG ammo

  4 Freezethrower ammo

  5 Chaingun, armor, Freezethrower ammo

* 6 Chaingun ammo

  7 RPG ammo, Healing Atom

  8 Chaingun, RPG ammo

  9 Medkit, chaingun ammo, blue key, Devastator ammo

10 Secret Room

11 Vantage point

12 Shotgun ammo, red key lock, Healing Atom

13 Blue key lock, yellow key, shotgun ammo, Devastator ammo, portable medkit, Freezethrower

14 Shotgun, yellow key lock, portable medkit

15 RPG ammo, pipebombs, Shrinker, Healing Atoms

*16 Jet pack

17 Night vision goggles, message: "The Crack Below."

18 Devastator ammo, chaingun, scuba tank

*19 Medkit, pistol, Shrinker ammo, Devastator

20 Devastator ammo, medkit

21 RPG ammo, Devastator ammo

22 Pipebombs, Holoduke, shotgun ammo, laser tripbombs, steroids

23 Red key

24 Shotgun ammo, RPG ammo, Devastator ammo, medkit

*25 Medkits

26 Chaingun ammo, Devastator ammo, Healing Atom, End

    *Denotes secret place

Pool of Blood

1   Check behind you for scuba gear and a large medkit as the mission begins. Remember our caution: if you have any air tank at all, it's best to come back for this one later. Octabrains patrol the tunnels ahead, between you and daylight. In the alcove on the right of the tunnel is an RPG cannon, and in a nook on the other side of the stone pillar are shotgun shells.

2   On the ledge outside the cave rests a large medkit and a pistol. Claiming them draws the attention of Enforcers and drones on a rooftop nearby, but the distance is easily enough to give you the advantage. Too bad there isn't a barrel handy for your trip over the falls....

3   Head for the bottom, mindful of sharks nearby—ammo for the RPG lies around the corner to the left. Don't surface in the same area you find the ammo, or you'll draw unwanted attention. Come back up near the falls, grab the night vision goggles at the waterline against the building, and proceed until you near the overhang.

4   Just inside the crevasse below you is Freezer ammo, and a pack of sharks rushing to its doom. When you've turned the fish to chum, surface again and activate the jetpack.

5   Fly low to the water and round the corner to the right. Slightly above you is a cave with a pair of Aliens and a chaingun. But it's what's below you that's most significant—a nasty Octabrain and pod cluster. From this position, lace the water below with pipebombs and detonate. Note that there's a secret place accessible from this ledge.

   Most of the Octabrain survive your assault, but if you take a running leap off the cliff, you'll submerge slightly when you hit the water. Drop Holoduke, swim, spin, and unload. In the area you mined previously rests naught but Armor and freezer ammo. When you're through, retreat quickly to the area on the other side of the overhang, near where you picked up that freezer ammo, previously. Submerge again and clean up the last of the sharks. When you surface, it's possibly you'll have drawn attention from a nearby Assault Commander, and perhaps even drones. They'll have a tough time targeting you as you float under the ledge—though you're homicidal efforts will be unimpaired. You might also engage the Aliens on the rooftop near water level. You're headed in their direction.

6   Secret Place. Open the window nearest the back of the cave to claim more chaingun ammo.

7   Submerge and approach the underwater cavern you see as you exit the crevasse. Inside the cave are the last two Octabrain you have to worry about for awhile, and more RPG ammo and a Healing Atom. The point where you find the Healing Atom is where you want to surface, and you had better come up dealing death.

8   A serious bunch of Aliens waits near the waterline (and one snipes from the cliff above). Once you've made a beach head, you'll find a chaingun and ammo for the RPG nearby.

9   On the huge steps leading up from where you find that RPG ammo, you'll collect a large medkit, ammo for the chaingun, then finally the blue key and two boxes of ammo for the Devastator. Don't engage the rooftop Enforcers far to your right just yet; in a few minutes you'll have a much better angle. Jump through the opening ahead and continue on the path after visiting the secret place.

10 Secret place. A small empty room, suitable for sniping, over-looks the blue key ledge.

11 Hide in the hallway and fight an uphill battle against Sentry Drones and Assault Commanders. Don't go out onto the roof until you're ready to answer a withering assault.

12 Stick to the left as you emerge on the rooftop. Far to the right, a cave starts puking forth Assault Commanders, drones and even a Boss Monster. There's a rooftop full of Enforcers down below, so stay back a ways while you deal with the first wave.

Drop back and hammer the Assault Commanders with RPG or Devastator. The Boss Monster comes leaping out of his cave, running in your direction, but he'll be forced to stop at the edge of the building below. Once the Assault Commanders have been sanctioned, move into position so that you can just see the head and shoulders of the Boss Monster on the top of the parapet below. In that way, you can use repetitive small arms fire to take care of him.

Finally, deal with any remaining Enforcers on the rooftop across the way. On your rooftop is a box of shotgun shells, as well as the red key lock. There's also a Healing Atom atop the sign below. Grab it and drop quickly into the water to avoid nearby Aliens and drones. Mark this spot, but swim back (no need to submerge!) to the falls before you turn and face the drones. That done, jet pack up and grab the air tank, if you haven't already. Below the spot where you hit the water after getting that Healing Atom is the blue key lock.

13 This room can be a real-lung burner. It's just one room, but it's full of Octabrains and pods. Praise the gods of 3D games for Holoduke. The objective is the yellow key at the bottom of the room, amidst the pods. There's also ammo for the shotgun and Devastator, a portable medkit, and a Freezer, for those Duke enough to make a pass before exiting. Realize that killing the chicks ushers in Octabrain, so you might want to tone down the artillery once you're inside the room. Conserve the air tank, and make your way back to the yellow key lock, near the falls.

14 Facing away from the falls, turn to your left and submerge just slightly. You should see an open window in the building. Inside are a pair of Octabrain, a shotgun and the yellow key lock. You can also surface in that room to claim a portable medkit. Use the yellow key and head upstairs.

15 Stop! Don't jump on the ventilation system or explore the other half of the roof yet! Big nasty traps ahead! OK—proceed. On the first half of the rooftop, slay any straggling Enforcers. You'll find ammo for the RPG, as well as pipebombs. A Shrinker rests on the ledge over the side of the building, as does a Healing Atom. Another Healing Atom sits in the cave above. In the back of that cave, the wall slides away to reveal a secret place.

16 Secret Place. Greetings, Mr. Jet pack! Come to Dukeboy! With the caveat that, if you still have plenty, it's best to be conservatice with the juice.

17 When you jump on top of the ventilation system, the wall of the canyon across from you blows to unleash a serious squad of Assault Commanders. Use the large vent structure for cover to pick them off on your own terms, and watch for any that wait below the roof line out of your sight. An Enforcer also appears on the ledge to your right. Once the coast is

clear, jet pack over to the Assault Commanders' cave. Inside is a pair of night vision goggles, and if you use them in the darkened area you'll read the message, "The Crack Below." If you toss a pipebomb from this cave and detonate, you'll open up a huge underwater cavern.

18 Drop down from the cave above and sink to the bottom. A school of sharks confronts you beneath the water, where you'll also find Devastator ammo, chaingun ammo and (YES!) another scuba tank. Surface to explore a truly huge secret place.

19 Secret Place. Hammer the far ledge as soon as you pop up: it's crawling with Octabrain and pods. There's also a large medkit, pistol and Shrinker ammo, and a Devastator in the wall nook.

20 Now, where were we? Ah, yes—the rooftop. After you finished the side trip, you're ready for the second part of the roof area. Sprint over and grab the Devastator ammo and large medkit, as another wall blows apart across the canyon. Inside are Assault Commanders and a Boss Monster. By now, you know the drill: deal with the Assault Commanders first, then take advantage of wherever the big ape ends up, somewhere below your vantage point.

21 Inside the cave that opens up you'll find ammo for both the RPG and Devastator.

22 Downstairs, break up the Octabrain convention and claim pipebombs, Holoduke, shotgun ammo, and a pair of laser tripbombs. There's also a stash of 'roids in the broken elevator. Throw the switch on the wall when you're ready for the red key: the windows open and the sign on the building rises to reveal your prize.

23 Claim the red key, dispatch any nearby sharks or Octabrains, and head for the red key lock.

24 Access the red key lock and slay the Enforcers. Expect Octabrain interference when you gather the shotgun shells and RPG ammo (behind the boxes) nearby. Across the water lies more ammo for RPG and Devastator, as well as a small medkit. Pressing the "Hard Hat Area" sign on the box reveals a secret place.

25 Secret Place. A door appears in the side of the stack of boxes; inside, two Enforcers guard a pair of large medkits.

26 In the tunnel, in addition to Octabrains aplenty, you can gather chaingun ammo, Devastator ammo, and a Healing Atom. Drop down the shaft and survive a nasty laser turret attack to activate the end-of-the-level switch.

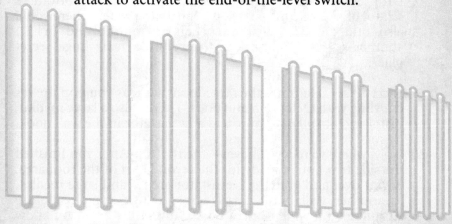

MISSION 4: L.A. RUMBLE

This mission isn't exactly mentally taxing... it's Duke as RPG sniper, battling the mean streets of La-La Land en route to bigger and better things.

Most of your foes try to wax you from a distance, and it's a good idea to return the favor. There's plenty of ammo about, so enjoy a little overkill, or you'll constantly be absorbing Pig Cop pellets. They seem remarkably able to peg you from about 500 meters, a luxury you can't enjoy without employing the RPG.

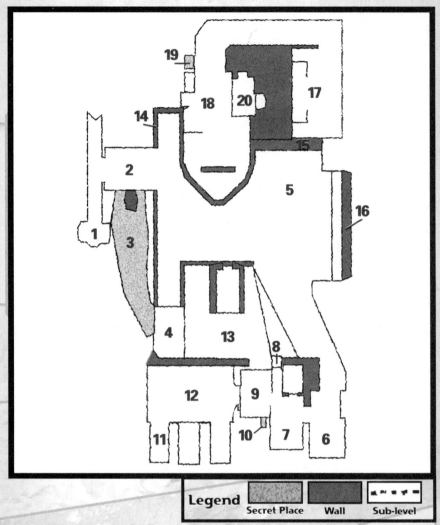

HIGHLIGHTS

- Three secret places
- Earthquake in Tinsel Town
- Duke 'copter ready for lift-off

MISSION 4: L.A. RUMBLE AT A GLANCE

  1 Shotgun ammo, medkit, pipebombs

  2 Shotgun ammo, weak wall

* **3** Freezethrower

  4 RPG ammo, RPG, medkits, Freezethrower ammo, shotgun ammo

  5 RPG ammo

  6 Medkit, pipebombs

  7 Pistol, medkit, night vision goggles, message: "Under the Knife."

  8 Medkit, Devastator ammo

  9 Blue key, steroids

***10** Healing Atom

 11 Devastator

 12 Devastator ammo

 13 Portable medkit

 14 Blue key lock, laser tripbombs, armor, medkit, RPG ammo

 15 Medkits, RPG ammo, shotgun ammo

 16 Healing Atoms, Shrinker

 17 Holoduke, medkit, Shrinker ammo

 18 Red key, medkit, jet pack, RPG, RPG ammo, Devastator ammo

***19** Devastator ammo

 20 Red key lock, teleporter to End

   *Denotes secret place

SHAKE IT, DUKEBOY

1   To your left as the mission begins rests a carton of shotgun shells, and on your right is a large medkit. The hall ahead looks dark and scary.... At the far end is naught but a box of pipebombs.

2   Kill the Pig Cop from afar and collect more shotgun ammo. Then try out those pipebombs on the weak wall to your right.

3   Secret place. The wall disintegrates nicely. A Freezethrower rests in the ruins. This back way provides the best entrance to the courtyard outside.

4   Slay the Enforcers and tend to the distant Pig Cops. Don't be afraid to defoliate the tree. The street is suddenly crawling with vermin, and the ledges of nearby buildings have their fair share, as well. In the area of the dearly departed Enforcers, gather up ammo for the RPG, an RPG itself, both a large and a portable medkit, and ammo for the Freezer and shotgun.

5   To gain access to the buildings, you'll have to run the gauntlet. Pig Cops take potshots from above as you navigate the avenue, pausing only briefly to scoop up another load of RPG ammo.

6   Bear right. The street dead-ends in a herd of Pig Cops harassing a hooker, and you should expect more swine to follow you down the alley. Clean the street of scum, and collect a large medkit and pipebombs before venturing through the open door.

7   A pistol rests just inside the door, where two Aliens make their last stand. In the Aliens' office is a large medkit and also night vision goggles. Using the goggles on the darkened wall nearby reveals the cryptic clue, "Under the Knife."

8   As you leave the office, check the wall to your right for a panel that slides to reveal another large medkit and ammo for the Devastator.

9   Expect company in the form of two Enforcers when you enter the room with the blue key. There's also a prescription

of steroids in the wall panel, and searching the cupboard under the knife reveals a secret place.

10 Secret place. Climb in and grab the Healing Atom.

11 Detonating the wall in room (9) causes some serious dismay in the local Pig Cop community... pain them further, then check the service elevators at your left. The far one holds a Devastator, the near one is functional, and quite plush.

12 Two Aliens and a mean wall turret preside over more Devastator ammo, while an Assault Commander in the shaft nearby begs for you to dispense some. Lucky Dukeboy!

13 Make a quick pass of the roof area and sprint back inside for cover—as soon as you explore the left side, an Assault Commander materializes above you. Clearing the area of Aliens and drones nets a portable medkit. Afterward, pause and lob shells into some of the windows nearby.

14 Sadly, the blue key opens the building you just ravaged. But now that the street is relatively free of filth, you can run back and pick up the laser tripbombs and the Armor off of the ledge below the big screen. Whaddaya know—an L.A. Rumble.... There's also a large medkit on the street nearby.
    To clean the ledge on the other side of the street, jump across the tunnel near where you found the Freezer ammo and portable medkit at the beginning of the mission. Watch for Drones, and be prepared for a backside Enforcer assault when you complete the tunnel leap. As you make your way along the ledge, pick up more RPG ammo, and use it on the Enforcers sniping from a distance.

15 As you step on the lighted ledge further along, an Assault Commander pains you from above. Punish him, and collect two large medkits, more RPG ammo, and two boxes of shotgun ammo. Now return to the rooftop of the blue key building.

16 From the rooftop, leap across the street to the small landing area with the Healing Atoms. Watch your step, and grab a Shrinker in addition to whatever the snipers have left behind. Make your way across the screen, hopscotching to and through the open window.

17 Blast the Aliens, and dispatch the Assault Commander who appears outside the window. There's also an Enforcer lurk-

ing up ahead. When the room is rid of alien refuse, collect Holoduke, a small medkit, and ammo for the Shrinker.

18 Upstairs, the remains of your target practice from across the street stage a desperate last stand. Expect a Pig Cop and Aliens, and perhaps even an Enforcer or two. In the room, you'll come across the red key, a large medkit, a jet pack and an RPG cannon. In the cabinet is ammo for both RPG and Devastator, and searching one of the nearby paintings yields a secret place.

19 Secret place. The painting to your right as you enter the room slides away to reveal a secret place containing Devastator ammo.

20 Press the button on the desk, partially hidden by the chair, to open the office nearby. Inside, Aliens and an Enforcer protect the red key lock. Once it's been accessed, the cabinet slides away to reveal a teleporter. You're bird's on the pad, Nukem....Whaddaya waitin' for?

MISSION 5: MOVIE SET

Sylvester. Arnold. Jean Claude. Sissies. This is making movies the Nukem way—no need for blank rounds or fake blood. And what is it with those alien bastards and the Duke ride?

This mission is actually pretty tame, with only one significantly brutal monster ambush to speak of. And of course, we'll show you how to take the sting out of even that. There is the entrance to the first Secret Mission of Episode Three: Tier Drops, as an added bonus.... Whenever you're ready: Roll 'em!

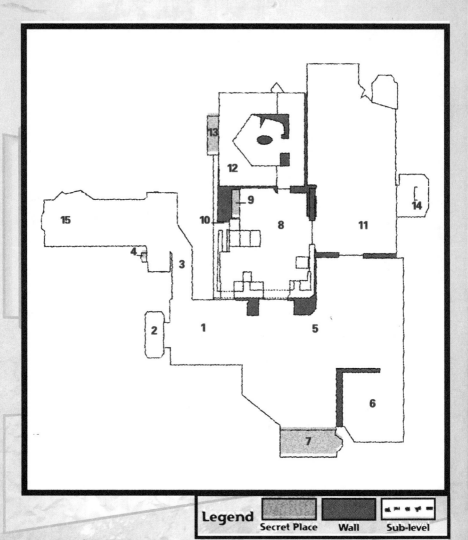

Legend

Secret Place	**Wall**	**Sub-level**

HIGHLIGHTS

- Four Secret Places
- Secret Level switch

MISSION 5: MOVIE SET AT A GLANCE

1 Medkit, shotgun ammo, shotgun
2 Portable medkit
3 Pistol, blue key, night vision goggles
* **4** Healing Atoms
5 Pistol ammo, Devastator ammo, pipebombs
6 Medkits, Freezethrower ammo, steroids
* **7** Healing Atom, freezer, Devastator ammo
8 Blue key lock, Devastator ammo, Healing Atom, medkit
* **9** Devastator
10 RPG ammo
11 Yellow key, chaingun, chaingun ammo, jet pack, pistol ammo,
pipebombs, portable medkit, Healing Atom, Secret Mission switch
12 Yellow key lock, medkits, Healing Atom, RPG, Shrinker ammo,
red key, night vision goggles
* **13** Jet pack, Shrinker, Healing Atom
14 Red key lock, switch, laser tripbombs, night vision goggles
15 Portable medkit, End

*Denotes secret place

Lights! Camera! Nukem!

1   Grab the large medkit beside you and about face, Nukem. Handle the parking garage before tackling the street. Take the shotgun shells and be ready for that window to pop open when you pick up the shotgun.

2   Pig Cops and an Enforcer guard a portable medkit. The cash register on the right is significant, as you'll soon see.

3   More Pig Cops and an Enforcer patrol the darkened hallway, unless, of course, you pause near the corner and lob a few pipebombs to your left.... On the ground is a pistol and the blue key. Using the night vision goggles, you find atop the soda machine reveals a reference to the previously noted cash register.

4   Secret place. Back in room (2), search the right register, then 'roid up and run back to room (3). The "Snacks" machine on the right slides to reveal an awesome stash of Healing Atoms.

5   Back in the street, advance from the garage until you hear the Pig Cops behind you, and take them out before continuing. Around the corner to your right are a swarm of Sentry Drones and an Assault Commander. By edging out, you can draw the attention of the first two drones, then deal with fatso on more reasonable terms. In the street you'll find ammo for the pistol and Devastator, as well as a box of pipebombs.

6   Exploring the crater left by your crashing 'copter yields two large medkits, Freezer ammo, and steroids. There's also a small medkit on the ledge above the 'roids, and from there you can jump to the sill of the Duke Nukem billboard.

7   Secret place. Walk through the triangular 3D Realms emblem to enter a secret place. A Healing atom, Freezer, and ammo for the Devastator are close at hand, and don't be shy about unloading a few rounds on the Assault Commander that shows up outside.

8   Accessing the blue key lock opens a room guarded by an Enforcer and a Pig Cop, and those two wall-mounted turrets bear mentioning, as well. Also, the bay door to your right

opens as you advance, admitting a trio of Aliens soon to be deceased. There's Devastator ammo on the ground, and you can reach the Healing Atom by standing atop the cameras. There's also a small medkit on another stack of boxes, and acquiring the shotgun ammo brings the sound of a sliding panel nearby.

9 Secret place. The sliding panel can also be activated by standing at the base of the big four-wide stack of boxes. Stand to the right and search, and a compartment above opens with a Devastator—and also a flock of Drones. Once the Drones are dealt with, the easiest way inside is a quick bit of jet pack.

10 Exploring the vent system, and wading through the Slimers therein, nets you a big box of RPG ammo, and also gives you a chance to soften up the crowd in the next room. In fact, if you enter through the vent, you get to deal with the upcoming enemies in two waves—highly recommended.

11 Drop down from the vent and slay the Pig Cops and Enforcers. Scouring the set turns up the yellow key, a chaingun and ammo, a jet pack, pistol ammo, pipebombs and a portable medkit...talk about the excesses of Hollywood... don't forget the Healing Atom on the ledge encircling the set. Note the humming coming from the space station. Hmmmm....

   When you step on the threshold of the door from room (8), two more Enforcers materialize, and the door to the street opens to admit Pig Cops and an Assault Commander. Let's see, now where did I put those laser tripbombs?

12 The room accessed by the yellow key features a seriously disadvantaged Enforcer reception committee. Situated as they are, below a ledge on either side of the set proper, they tend to leap harmlessly up and down while you devise cruel means of executing them. Gosh, that fire extinguisher is positioned conveniently.... There's a large medkit nearby, and blowing the extinguisher reveals a nook holding a Healing Atom. Inside the spaceship you can collect an RPG, ammo for the Shrinker, a small medkit, and also the red key. When seated near the red key, search the map display to open a compartment to your left containing night vision goggles. Did we forget to mention the secret place?

13 Secret place. Stand in front of the large Earth mural, jump up and forward—you enter a room with a jet pack and a Shrinker. If you explore the duct above, you'll find a Healing Atom, and a switch that connects that part of the ventilation system to the rest.

14 Utilizing the red key opens a small unguarded room. Entering the room triggers the arrival of a Boss Monster outside, just in case you thought the mission was too damn easy.... Throw the lever on the console to move the obstruction you saw earlier, and grab the laser tripbombs and night vision goggles off the top of the computer before you run outside to deal with big ugly.

> ## Tip!
> Before you throw the end-of-the-level switch in the last room, perhaps you'd like to visit the nearby Secret Level? Press on the large USA sign on the side of the space station (remember the humming?) and the side wall now lifts to reveal the button to Tier Drops.

15 As you near the bottom of the steps, a series of explosions seals the tunnel behind you, and Aliens stage an ambush. Collect the portable medkit when things have calmed down a little, and hit the switch.

MISSION 6: RABID TRANSIT

This is a sweet little bit of Nukem. And it is a little bit. The Rabid Transit scenario isn't big on encounter areas, but in each there's a considerable amount of stuff to see and do. The two major traps are even pretty diabolical, though there's enough ammo and supplies lying about that you don't really have to spend a lot of time with tactical analysis. Point and shoot, Dukester. Some things never change.

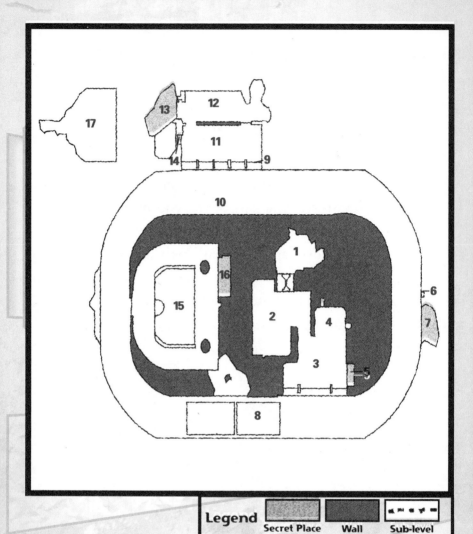

Legend	Secret Place	Wall	Sub-level

HIGHLIGHTS

- Six Secret Places
- Speeding subway splattering
- One extremely phallic secret room

MISSION 6: RAPID TRANSIT AT A GLANCE

  1 Shotgun ammo, shotgun, medkit
  2 Medkits, pipebombs, night vision goggles
  3 Shotgun ammo, medkits, pipebomb, Healing Atom
* 4 Holoduke
* 5 Chaingun
  6 Devastator
* 7 Healing Atom, steroids, Devastator ammo
  8 Chaingun, Healing Atom, RPG, portable medkit
  9 Laser tripbombs, medkit
10 Blue key, Armor, portable medkit
11 Blue key lock, pistol, medkit
12 Red key, Healing Atom, Devastator ammo, chaingun ammo
*13 Freezethrower ammo, RPG ammo, Devastator
*14 RPG ammo
15 Red key lock, Shrinker ammo, pipebombs, Devastator ammo
*16 Medkits, Devastator ammo, RPG ammo
17 Shrinker, medkits, End

    *Denotes secret place

Subway to Hell

1   Behind you, as the mission begins, a stash of shotgun ammo awaits. A shotgun rests in the ruins just ahead, near a large medkit.

2   Take out the two nasty turrets near the magazine shop and slay the Alien that appears. When you start browsing the shelves, expect a rush of Pig Cops and Aliens from the train area. Nearby, you'll discover a small and a large medkit, a box of pipebombs, and, if you search the cash register, a section of shelf drops to reveal a compartment with night vision goggles.

3   In the boarding area, stay on guard for lurking Pig Cops as you collect ammo for the shotgun and a small medkit. More shotgun ammo and a large medkit are hidden in the trashcans, and the snack machine holds both the obvious pipebomb and a Healing Atom—search the machine to make your selection....

4   Secret place. If you hop on the left-hand magazine rack, then hop back off again, a compartment holding Mr. Holoduke is disclosed.

5   Secret place. The Duke Nukem billboard slides upward to reveal a secret place holding a chaingun. Hop inside to claim your prize, and the drone bearing down on your backside will explode harmlessly against the wall.

6   Go ahead and deal with the laser tripbombs, but don't take the train yet. Instead, let both trains pass, then run behind them. You'll spy a panel in the right-hand wall that opens to reveal a Devastator. You can safely cling in that niche as the trains pass. When they've gone by again, step out and discover a secret place.

7   Secret place. To the right of the Devastator niche is a weak spot in the wall. Blasting it creates a cavern with a Healing Atom, steroids, and ammo for the Devastator. When you're quite through, let the trains pass and hurry back to the station.

8   All Aboard! The cars on one train hold a chaingun cannon and a Healing Atom, while the other has an RPG and a portable medkit as passengers.

9 Disembark and kill the Pig Cops. A major laser tripbomb haul is your reward, along with a large medkit. From this vantage point, slay the Enforcers on the ledge you can see to your right.

10 Jump to the ledge (from the train) now littered with Enforcer parts and claim the blue key. There's also Armor and a portable medkit within reach. Ride the train back around to where you previously peppered Pig Cops to put the key to use.

11 Slay the squad of Pig Cops in the room beyond the blue key lock and gather a pistol and a large medkit.

12 The darkened area ahead is an intriguing little Duke trap. The room is inhabited by Octabrains and full of pods. Fortunately, the pods are laced with explosives. Unfortunately, when the charges go off, more Octabrain show up outside. Add to that the Assault Commander lurking up ahead, and the two Boss Monsters...things get hairy in a hurry.

First, drop Holoduke in the outside area, about halfway down the room. Duck inside and blow the pods, then return and break up the party harassing Holoduke.

Notice that the wall has been blown away (right in the middle of your own damn poster... good thing Duke Nukem doesn't believe in bad omens). Peeking in the hole, you can get the Assault Commander's attention without even trying. He'll happily come outside to get stepped on.

Also draw out the first Boss Monster in the same fashion, though it's preferable to kill him while he's still in the room. You won't last long otherwise. Use the Devastator—in these small quarters, there's no room for finesse. Jump in the hole and advance towards the room's main entrance. The second Boss materializes in the left corner of the room, and he comes in gunning.

When it's all over, the red key is yours, as well as a Healing Atom and ammo for the Devastator. If you shoot the trashcan outside, you'll discover ammo for the chaingun therein. And if you press on the wall at the opposite end of the room from where you found the key, you'll discover a secret place.

13 Secret place. Inside the room is ammo for the Freezer, and a switch on the control console that reveals something, well... downright graphic. Killing the chicks calls Octabrains, just

in case you're unclear on the concept. In the piston room is more ammo for the RPG, and also a Devastator weapon.

14 Secret place. Before you run off, search the mail box and a panel slides open above it. Climb inside for RPG ammo.

15 The red key lock opens the door on another world of hurt, but Dukeman has a much better chance of coming out of this one relatively unscathed. Dodge quickly to one side as you enter, avoiding fire from two Assault Commanders in the room's central chamber. There's also a Boss Monster down there, which is where you'd like to keep him. Don't run too far down either ramp, or he'll chase you in the perimeter.

You should be able to peek over the top of the wall near where you came in, and peg the Boss Monster with small arms fire. The Assault Commanders will hover below you on the other side of the wall, as is their way. When the Boss Monster finally succumbs, then walk down a ramp and draw out the Commanders for a little high-stepping fun.

Granting the chick's request ushers in three Octabrains, so you might think about setting a pipebomb beside her, then dropping Holoduke before you hurry to a vantage point near the bookshelves.

Inside the box in the room is ammo for the Shrinker, and there's also a box of pipebombs nearby.

Blast the large vase, and a niche in the wall holding Devastator ammo is revealed. While you're blasting, take out the weak spot in the wall, to the right of the bookcases. There's nothing in the fissure. Hey, sometimes, Duke's just gotta blast.

Oh all right... jump on the wall you've just created, and from there to the top of the closest bookshelf. At the end of the other bookshelf is a Healing Atom, and the Enforcers rushing your way came from a secret place.

16 Secret place. Inside the room behind the bookcase are three large medkits, two boxes of ammo for the Devastator and also a box of refills for the RPG. Happy, Dukeboy?

17 Below the water are three Octabrains and a Shrinker, and the tunnel to the end-of-the-level switch. Near the switch are a couple of large medkits, not that you should need them....

MISSION 7: FAHRENHEIT

The Fahrenheit experience is a tidy little exploration of a few city streets and buildings, with most areas designed to sucker you into a larger firefight than you bargain for. Be a sneaky Duke, drawing the battle to you, and there's little to be concerned with.

Getting to the end-of-the-level switch is a bit of a doozy, as you battle two Boss Monsters and an Enforcer goon squad while you're treading water. Hang on to that Devastator ammo—it most definitely comes in handy.

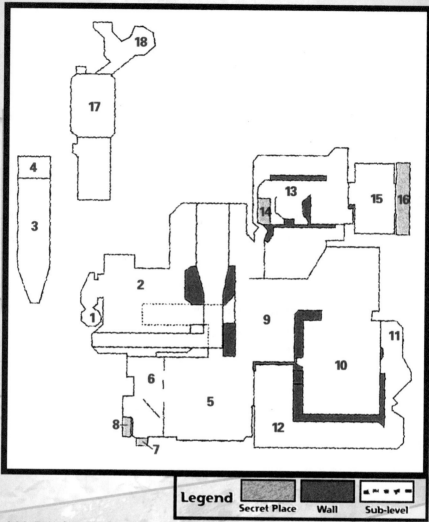

Legend   Secret Place   Wall   Sub-level

HIGHLIGHTS

- Four Secret Places
- Several major firefights
- Grim Boss Monster trap

Mission 7: Fahrenheit At a Glance

1 Medkits
2 Shotgun ammo, pipebombs, pistol, chaingun ammo, medkits
3 Shotgun, Shrinker
4 Red key lock, shotgun ammo, portable medkit, blue key
5 Blue key lock, Armor, Healing Atom, medkit, portable medkit, Devastator ammo
6 RPG ammo, Devastator ammo, steroids, night vision goggles, laser tripbomb
* 7 Freezethrower
* 8 Portable medkit
9 Medkit, shotgun ammo
10 Portable medkit, Holoduke, shotgun ammo
11 Shrinker ammo, Healing Atom, shotgun ammo
12 RPG, yellow key
13 Laser tripbomb, Devastator
*14 Red key
15 Chaingun, chaingun ammo
*16 Healing Atom, Freezethrower ammo
17 RPG cannon
18 Medkits, End

*Denotes secret place

Hot Shots

1   Two large medkits sit behind you as the mission gets under-
    way. To exit the area, press on the side of the dumpster that
    blocks the opening, and it swings aside.

2   Pig Cops and Aliens patrol this area. Hopping up on the
    dumpster's edge gives you a good shot at the first few trou-
    blemakers, though the room to your left is full of foes. Once
    things quiet down, you can check nearby for shotgun shells,
    a box of pipebombs, a pistol, and chaingun ammo. A large
    medkit and two small medkits are in the vicinity, and there's
    also another stash of shotgun ammo in one of the trashcans.
    The blue key lock adorns the door at the bottom of the
    walkway.

3   Jump in the stream near where you dropped that first Pig
    Cop and ride the current. When you make the small drop-
    off, submerge and dispatch the three Octabrains in the dis-
    tant underwater alcove. Behind you in the wall rests a shot-
    gun, and there's also a Shrinker up ahead.

4   Surface where you find the Shrinker and you'll be in a small
    room near the red key lock. Also in attendance: more shot-
    gun ammo, a portable medkit, and the blue key.

5   Accessing the blue key lock grants entry to a nasty little
    room of stacked boxes, full of Aliens and drones and
    presided over by Pig Cop snipers. Pick up the armor near
    the doorway, and advance with caution. One drone usually
    spots you in the hall—detonate it from a distance with
    chaingun. Peek out to your right and blast the Alien at
    ground level, then use RPG to clean the windows above of
    the snipers.
        Standing in the hallway, move straight ahead into the open
    area until someone spots you, then back up into the hall and
    lie in wait. In this way, you can take out the Aliens and
    drones on this side of the room. When the drone humming
    is no longer evident, exit the hall and quickly take a position
    in the far left corner of the room. There's turrets above that
    peg you if you stay near the hallway exit.
        From there, run along the wall to your left and draw out
    more Drones and Aliens. Finally circle back and take out the
    turrets and the lone remaining Alien, on the stacks to the left
    of the single box near where you came in.

Climb the boxes and leap to the sill of the snipers' window. If you explore the tops of the boxes right now, you'll start another battle.

6   Kill any straggler Pig Cops. When you enter the room, an Assault Commander appears outside in the hallway near where you picked up the armor. It's easiest to run down there and shrink him, then return to this room. There's another Commander nearby, as you can so plainly hear, but he's not a current threat. In the Pig pad you'll find RPG ammo, Devastator ammo, steroids, night vision goggles, and a laser tripbomb. There's even some big screen entertainment.... Taking out the weak wall puts you back where you started, but don't go yet.

7   Secret Place. Searching the large painting on the wall puts you face to face with a Freezer, and also a pair of laser turrets. Yowch! Some secrets are better left untold....

8   Secret Place. Using the night vision goggles on the darkened wall reveals the message, "Blast the Bottles." Once you do so, simply walk through the cabinet and enter another secret place, this one containing a portable medkit.
        Searching area (5) thoroughly yields several goodies, as well as an opposing viewpoint on the O.J. verdict.... Gather up a Healing Atom, large medkit, portable medkit, and ammo for the Devastator. Be ready for Aliens and drones at any time. They'll come from that opening between the two walls. If you stand where you pick up the Devastator ammo, most of the drones and Enforcers in the next area oblige by standing below you, on the other side of the wall. You might want to point out the tactical disadvantages of this situation to them before continuing. You can also line up a long-distance RPG shot from here to remove a wall-mounted laser turret.

9   Open the iron door near where you found the armor earlier and take care of any remaining drones. If you went so far as to take out the turret previously, the coast is probably pretty clear. Shooting the trashcans near the large medkit yields more shotgun ammo, and if you go near the yellow keylocked door, a pair of Enforcers attempt to punish your idle curiosity.

10 Advance on the Fire Station with care. As you near the garage bay, two Enforcers leap the wall on your left and

attack. Unless you back up to dispose of them, you end up in a nasty crossfire between them and the load of Pig Cops in the station itself.

Run past the front of the fire truck and slay the swine around that side, then pop back and RPG the knot of Cops gathered together for ease of disposal. Behind the panel is a portable medkit, and that's no light fixture—it's Holoduke atop the fire truck, keeping company with more shotgun shells.

11 Blowing the weak spot on the wall nearby initiates a real pork roast, if all those shotguns scattered nearby are any indication. On the steps you'll find Shrinker ammo, a Healing Atom, and more shotgun shells. Up top, expect to hear the golden tones of Assault Commanders as you round the corner. Drop back and wait for them to come relieve you of some of those Shrinker charges.

12 Scoop up the RPG cannon in the hallway. In the room ahead, another Assault Commander makes his last stand between you and the yellow key. The switch on the wall lowers the key for ease of access, and also provides a shortcut back to the Fire Station.

13 As previously reported, you can expect Enforcer trouble as you approach the yellow key lock. More wait just inside the door, while upstairs there's a serious Alien infestation in need of quick death. Searching the control center turns up a laser tripbomb, a Devastator weapon, and the entrance to a secret place.

14 Secret Place. The iron door at the back of the room opens to reveal three Aliens and the red key. Give them some constructive criticism with regards to choosing a secret location....

15 An Assault Commander and an Enforcer engaging in whimsical talk show banter need to have their show canceled, Duke style. Collect a chaingun and some additional ammo, and when you're done playing DJ, step through the curtain to find a secret place.

16 Secret Place. Walking through the red curtain puts you in a room with a Healing Atom and Freezer ammo.

17 Accessing the red key lock opens up one of the nastiest logistical problems yet for the Dukemind. You're sure to take

some damage from the two Boss Monsters and horde of Enforcers beyond, what with nowhere to retreat but to the pool of water behind you.

The trick is to open the door standing slightly off to one side, and back quickly into the water. Submerge, then swim to the opposite corner of the room, near the back wall. When you come back up, you should be able to Devastate the room's contents into submission before they can properly respond.

The switch inside reveals an RPG cannon. After claiming it, blow the weak wall to proceed.

18 The cavern that opens up holds large medkits and the end-of-the-level switch.

MISSION 8: MOTEL HELL

One last "real" mission between here and the final show-down, Dukeboy. Play it real smart, so that you have all the goodies you need to turn back the Supreme Commander of the alien invasion.

The Motel is mostly about minor monsters in large numbers, materializing in such a way as to blast your backside a few times before you realize that the blood splattering that wall there is yours. Each time you even imagine you might be crossing a threshold, seek cover.

The Boss Monsters are pretty much at your mercy in the cozy confines of the Motel, though one does have a tendency to reach the street outside. Coax the big turds into a situation where they're tempted to fire into a wall, and thank god that they're not ambidextrous.

Hourly rates? Hell, this won't take that long....

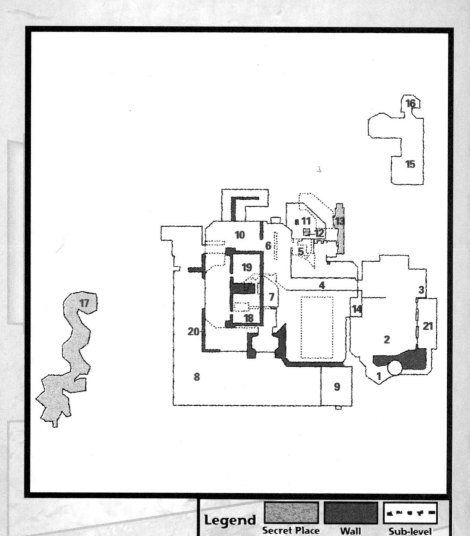

HIGHLIGHTS

- Three Secret Places
- Boss Monsters by poolside
- Indiana Jones dining on steak
- Button to Secret Mission: Freeways

MISSION 8: MOTEL HELL AT A GLANCE

1 Medkits

2 Blue key lock, pistol, pipebombs, shotgun ammo, chaingun ammo, medkit, chaingun, portable medkit

3 Chaingun ammo, steroids, shotgun ammo, blue key

4 Exploding bathroom

5 Medkits, RPG, Devastator ammo

6 Medkit, Shrinker ammo, RPG ammo

7 Medkits, shotgun ammo, portable medkit, Armor, night vision goggles, shotgun ammo

8 Shotgun ammo, medkit

9 Devastator, medkits, yellow key

10 Yellow key lock, Freezethrower ammo

11 Medkits

*12 Holoduke

*13 Portable medkit, scuba tank, pipebombs, Freezethrower

14 Pipebombs

15 Armor

16 Healing Atom

*17 Freezethrower, Healing Atoms, Indiana Jones, button for Secret Mission

18 Medkits, Armor, chaingun ammo

19 RPG ammo, medkit, Shrinker

20 Healing Atoms, Devastator ammo

21 Medkits, pipebombs, End

*Denotes secret place

SCUM CHECKS IN...

1   Peek through the slit in the enclosure to your right as the mission begins... say, is that a switch in there? Large medkits are also nearby.

2   The courtyard outside is soon to be crawling with Pig Cops—don't let the quiet fool you. In addition to the ones that show up at ground level, you can also expect snipers from above. Don't be afraid to dispense a little heavy artillery to even the odds. Scattered near the blue key lock (and stashed in trash cans) you'll collect a pistol, pipebombs, shotgun ammo, two boxes of ammo for the chaingun, and a large medkit. Don't forget to check the dumpster (and dispose of the diver). Inside is a chaingun and a portable medkit.

3   By climbing the fence you can leap across to the building. Near where you land you'll find more ammo for the chaingun, as well as a refill of 'roids. On the ledge above there's more shotgun ammo, and even the blue key. Watch for another Pig Cop and an Alien when you return to the blue key lock.

4   Pig Cops guard the hallway inside, and as you approach the lobby some kind of plumbing disaster takes out a good portion of the bathroom, along with a few assembled swine.

5   The bathroom lays in ruins. Avoid the displaced rat population and pound any Pig Cops that might have survived the blast. Inside, you'll find three large medkits, an RPG cannon, and a box of ammo for the Devastator.

6   Explore the lobby, but be careful going around the corner to the left. A couple of Boss Monsters are minding the front desk, which would explain why business is a little slow. In safer territory, you can grab up a large medkit, ammo for the Shrinker, and even that box of RPG ammo, if you're quick.

7   Get the Boss Monsters' attention, and then retreat to the lobby. If you move back and forth along that common wall, you'd be surprised how much damage a couple of those big monkeys can do to the room—and each other. With a little patience, you'll save big on ammo. Eventually, you'll have to

deal with one of them, but even he should be a shadow of his former self.

Entering the room calls in a pair of Enforcers from the direction of the front door. Next time, guys, call ahead for a reservation....

In the Boss Monsters' remains of a room, you'll discover a large medkit, shotgun ammo, and a portable medkit. There's also a sliding panel in the array of boxes closest to the door that reveals an armor vest, and activating the switch discloses a room containing night vision goggles.

In the lobby foyer beyond the front desk sits more shotgun ammo, and also a small medkit.

8   Return to the door marked "Exit" in the lobby and venture out back. Pig Cops are on the prowl, two in recon vehicles, so stay alert. There's shotgun ammo and a large medkit near the rear entrance. As you round the corner of the building, dust the second porcine jetcar and watch the windows at the end of the street. They'll open as you crest the rise, and Pig Cops and Enforcers pour out seconds later. Unless, of course, they're detained while they rattle around in the room with an RPG or three....

9   Inside the room, the Devastator sits on the table, and several large medkits top the bookshelves. Searching the picture reveals the yellow key, and also summons an Assault Commander. For added emphasis, try to shrink him outside, and do the flying jump-squish. See ya, tiny.

10   Accessing the yellow key lock in the hotel lobby opens both doors. Choose the stairway, slaying Pig Cops as you climb. At the top, a fresh supply of Freezer ammo lies unattended. From the doorway, slay the Enforcers at the desk to your left. More Pig Cops line the hall to your right, while the left avenue leads to the pool, and a couple more Boss Monsters.

This whole floor is pretty much run and shoot, from one encounter area to the next. Occasionally, you may have to go and forage for medkits you've left behind. The Boss Monsters are relatively easy prey in the small confines of the hotel. Just orient them so that their chaingunning into a wall, instead of your body, and a few RPG shots will do the trick. In addition to all the weapons and ammo your foes relinquish upon dying, you should also find:

11 In the area of the desk, you'll find two large medkits in each of the small refrigerators. There's also two secret places nearby.

12 Secret place. Behind the desk, search the wine rack and it lifts to reveal Holoduke.

13 Secret Place. To the right of the small refrigerators, the wall lifts to reveal a portable medkit, and a ramp leading up. At the top of the ramp is a panel containing an air tank and a box of pipebombs—now what could those be for? In the shark tank nearby is a Freezer—and all these little pieces of shark....

14 In the area of the pool, collect the pipebombs, and then jump up on the small landing above the "No Lifeguard..." sign. Three windows across the street open up, giving you a prime targeting angle on the Enforcers inside. Kill them now; you'll stop by to pay your respects later.

15 Underwater, three Octabrains guard an armor vest, and at that same end of the pool you may note a weak spot on the wall....

16 Blowing the pool wall gives access to a small underwater tunnel, which seems to dead-end in a tiny room. Look for the corner of the room which has brighter lighting, and surface there to grab the Healing Atom you saw in the bathroom so long ago.

17 Secret Place. Following the direction on the darkened wall near the pool leads to a bizarre encounter with Indiana Jones, and also the last Secret Level in Duke Nukem: Freeway. Check it out, but finish up this mission and double back, or you'll miss out on the goodies ahead in the hotel. Hop in the pool and venture through the fountain (really: a small waterfall).

Follow the cave until it comes to the mouth of another cave. There's a Freezer nearby. Press the hand print on the wall for access. Venture inside and follow the cave (a Secret Place) to its termination... Hey Indy! Stick around! When you grab the Healing Atoms, the cave starts to collapse a la **Raiders**. Beat it back outside. Did someone say Secret Level?

Look to the right of the cave you just exited. There seems to be a manhole cover on the ground.... If you defoliate the trees, you'll see the button to Freeways. Back to the hotel for now.

18 Circling around to the other hallway, the first door on your right houses Aliens and other more important things: two small medkits, armor, and ammo for the chaingun.

19 Further down the hall, Pig Cops preside over a box of ammo for the RPG, and a large medkit. In the duct connecting this room and the last lies a Shrinker.

20 Blowing the fire extinguishers in the hallway gives access to the ledge outside, where you can scoop up Healing Atoms and two boxes of ammo for the Devastator. Now head for that building across the street, where you saw the windows open from poolside.

21 The room itself is empty, but kick out the duct and follow it to the drop-off. Below are two large medkits, a box of pipebombs, and the end-of-the-level switch.

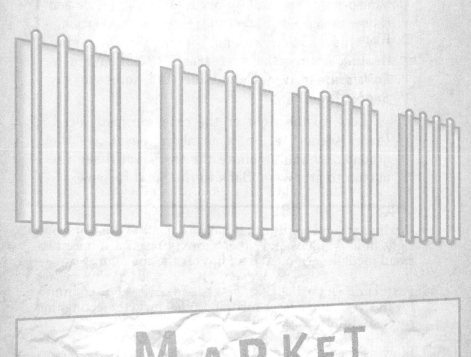

MISSION 9: STADIUM

THE BIG GAME

Finally, and with no small risk of personal health, Duke Nukem has purged the alien menace from our little corner of the solar system....

With one big, one-eyed freak of an exception.

It's down to Duke vs. Freak for world supremacy, and the Earth couldn't be in better hands.

It's not easy being Duke, and this final confrontation is no cakewalk. But when it comes to outwitting scum, you've already proven your prowess time and again. Too bad there's not a little more in the way of artillery on the field of play....

The following battle plan works about 80 percent of the time. The caveat is that the monster needs to score just one direct hit on you with his missiles, and you are Duke toast. But these tactics, applied with the skill and nerve that make Nukem who he is, at least give humanity a fighting chance.

☞ As the mission begins, you're rising through a cylinder, up to ground-level in a huge football arena. The monster will be right in front of you, and he won't take kindly to your assessment of his ocular abnormality. Don't wait for the platform to stop rising to activate your jet pack, and climb high into the sky as you hurl your challenge.

☞ Pan around and look for the blimp. One good RPG shot opens it wide up, littering the playing field with ammo and accessories of all types. Now your in business.

☞ Stay in the air except when you need to restock. We highly recommend the RPG to combat the giant creature.

☞ Fly at an altitude about half of what you're capable of, and keep an eye on the jet pack consumption. Only land when you're about out of jet pack juice, and when you land, do so with a refill of steroids right in front of you.

☞ As soon as you land, 'roid up. Run like crazy across the field, angling towards the RPG ammo, a new jet pack, and health boosts... and away from the big monster.

- If you hit a bottle of steroids while you're running in 'roid mode, you drop back out into regular speed. Avoid the jars of steroids as if they were land mines for that reason: If you drop back to normal speed on the playing field anywhere near the monster, he'll kill you.

- Once you're satisfied with your haul, take to the air again.

  As far as combat tactics go, there only seems to be one thing that works worth a damn the majority of the time, and that's strafing along the diagonal of the field. If you fly all the way to one corner, the monster follows you, but winds up about the middle of the field by the time you turn around to face him.

- Angle your shots downward, and let loose with the RPG as you pass relatively 40-50 meters over big ugly's head. As long as your weapon is targeted in front of him, the projectile evens out and catches him full-on. Keep firing until you're past him, and continue to the opposite corner of the field. Adjust your height once you've passed overhead to throw off anyone aiming at you, just be sure to strafe from roughly the same elevation. If you're too low, the monster blasts you just as if you were on the ground running right at him. If you're too high, you have to adjust your aim too quickly, and it's hard to get in a worthwhile number of shots per pass.

- Ignore the Aliens and Assault Commanders (which arrive when a cheerleader happens into the line of fire). Occasionally, you'll find it opportune to dispatch a lesser monster, and you can certainly afford some ammo to take them out. Just don't become distracted from the task at hand.

- While you're in the air, remember you can utilize the portable medkit. Your bound to catch some flack, and you're sure to get another portable medkit as soon as you're on the ground.

- Note that two Healing Atoms lie in each end zone.

Also note that the monster is capable of doing great damage to itself if it gets face first against a goal post, chasing you, and unloads big missiles. It's not a standard tactic, because the odds are that one of those missiles will make it around a post and upside your head. But the creature can be positioned so that it kills itself by absorbing its own blasts.

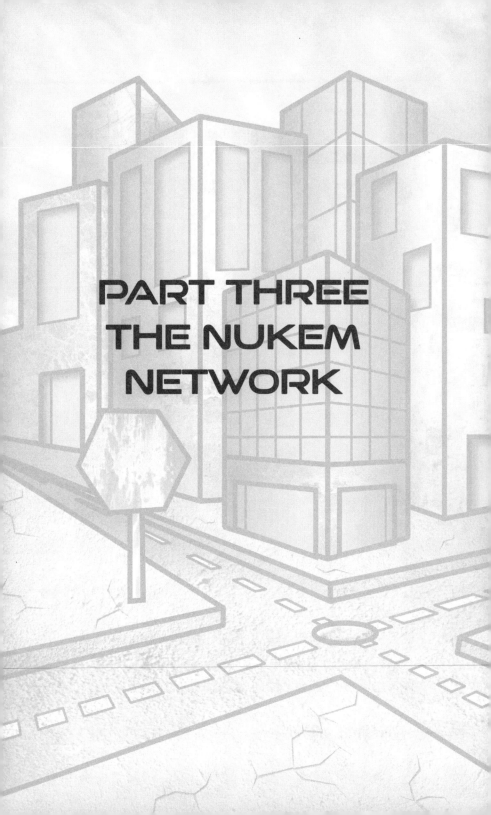

PART THREE
THE NUKEM
NETWORK

CHAPTER 7
KILLING YOUR FRIENDS LIKE A PRO

We don't know many people who prefer cooperative Dukematch over the down-n-dirty, kill-yer-buddy death-match play. We've done a lot of both, and inevitably find ourselves shooting each other in the back instead of ridding the world of those dastardly Aliens. We'll wager you'll do the same and for that reason the strategies we list here are specific for head-to-head play.

If you don't run, you're dead. The first thing you'll notice is that your human opponents move at an incredible rate. Because of this, all things are essentially equal. That is to say, the best Duke usually wins. If you're movement and fire strategies aren't sharp, precise, and almost second-nature, you'll be dead before you know it. If you don't know the lay of the landscape, you're also at a tremendous disadvantage. In short, the better your single-player skills, the more deadly you'll be in Dukematch.

Also, you're not some Alien or Pig Cop, so use the savvy your human brain affords you. In other words, be unpredictable and opportunistic (especially if you play against the same opponents a lot). Use Holoduke as a decoy; listen for gunfire and try to anticipate where your enemy is coming from, or where he's going; create distractions like opening doors or wasting a few rounds to make others think something's going on[Em]and when they come to investigate they'll walk right into your ambush; hide behind false walls (you can see them but they can't see you); and use light switches to hide in the shadows. Every professional hitman knows that there are countless ways to kill your buddies. You're only limitation is your creativity.

The number of players you have should dictate which mission landscape you use; the fewer players you have, the smaller the area you'll want to use as your venue. Otherwise you'll waste a lot of time just trying to find each other. We've also found that playing multiplayer with respawning monsters (the "Damn, I'm Good" setting) is a frantic blast—especially because Duke and all the weapons also respawn.

Even though the same tactics we describe in the beginning of the book apply in Dukematch play, some hard-hitting specifics are worth noting. They are:

- RPG rockets track targets that are in contact with the ground. So, if an RPG rocket is headed your way, you might as well jump—and jumping sideways is probably most effective. If you time your leap right, the rocket will sail harmlessly past you.

> **Tip!**
> If you can get close to your opponent, you can jump on his head. He'll think you vanished into thin air.

- Place pipebombs **behind** trash cans, ammo boxes, medkits, etc., and hide in wait. When your enemy comes in to grab the goods, detonate. Nasty.

- Try stepping into a room or corridor and immediately snapping back. Due to the game's frame-rate, your opponent(s) may be duped into thinking that you've actually run through the open area (they may not have seen you leap back). If your opponent gives chase (which they always seem to do), he'll be chasing a phantom and won't know what hit him when you shoot him from behind.

☞ Savvy Dukematch players think of teleporters as fancy doorways. Send pipebombs, RPG rockets, and about anything else through a teleport before you enter (or if you've escaped death via teleport, fire back through it. You never know what you might hit). Conversely, be careful not to hang out directly in front of a teleporter. You'll notice new teleporters and rooms in Dukematch play that aren't available in single player mode. It makes the game that much more dynamic and replayable.

EPISODE ONE, MISSION 7: FACES OF DEATH

This mission is a virtual blast, but you can't play it unless you're in multiplayer mode. To get a look at the faces of death (and get this pun), the Duke Master must select the first episode and then choose Mission 7.

The layout here is designed to confuse you (and even after you know the method to the madness, it's still confusing). What's more, there are tons of places to hide and not a lot of room to turn tail and run—making this the ultimate Dukematch mission. Knowing the quirks on this mission definitely puts you at an advantage, and here are the best we found:

☞ The teleporters take you in one large circle. When you are in the larger rooms, think of the teleporters as doorways that take you to a hidden alcove between two large rooms. Inside, you'll collect all kinds of swell ammo, items, and weapons.

☞ The streams of high-voltage in room (5) and (15) won't hurt you, though the pile-drivers will.

☞ Iris buttons: activate all of them in the mission (such that they are "open"), then access the key lock to open room (14). The last iris buttons in (14) open room (15)— which contains an RPG and a Devastator.

☞ The key lock in (13)—its on the left wall above the Todd's tank—opens every entrance into (14). Once someone opens this room, it can't be closed. Don't worry about finding a key; every Duke magically starts with one.

☞ You will take damage in the water tanks if someone shoots at you through a forcefield. In other words, water tanks don't make good hiding places.

☞ Many heavier weapons (the best are RPG rounds) can be fired into a teleporter and will fly through the teleporter to the next in an endless loop of death. If you do this, be careful not to get caught in your own trap. Eventually, if the shot is off-line at all, the round will hit the wall beside the teleporter.

☞ When you get into room (14), you can ride the waves and duck into the opening that leads to areas (17) and (18)—both are great hiding places with valuable prizes.

Whatever you do while running in circles in this elaborate hamster wheel is up to you; however, don't forget to be creative, ruthless, and have fun.

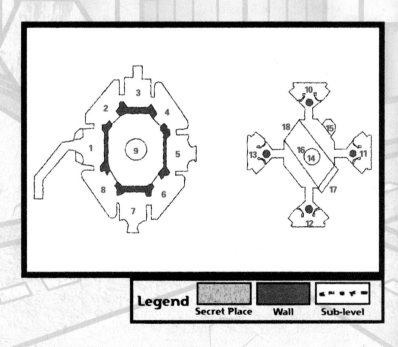

Legend

Secret Place   Wall   Sub-level

MISSION 7: FACES OF DEATH AT-A-GLANCE

We've numbered the rooms so that we could easily label the map. However, we recommend that you focus on the face names or events within each area, and play the association game (i.e., use them as cairns in you hike through carnage). For clarity, we've only used the names above and inside the water tanks.

Follow this numbered map by starting in the Lava Flow Room and go left

1 Lava Flow Room. RPG ammo (Todd), chaingun ammo (Allen)
2 Lava Waterfall. Medkit, left teleport to (13) (Allen/Todd), right teleport to (10) (Greg/Richard)
3 Fire Room. Shotgun ammo (Greg), iris button, pipebombs (Richard)
4 Moon Room. Medkit, left teleport to (10) (Greg/Richard), right teleport to (11) (James/Dirk)
5 Electric Column Room. Two boxes of Shrinker ammo (James & Dirk), iris button
6 Lava Waterfall. Medkit, left teleport to (11) (James/Dirk), right teleport to (12) (Chuck/Steve)
7 Empty Room. Freezer ammo (Chuck), iris button, Devastator ammo (Steve)
8 Earth Room. Medkit, left teleporter to (12) (Chuck/Steve), right teleporter to (13) (Todd/Allen)
9 Center Room (You can jump to the platform without 'roids). Medkits, armor, boots, night vision goggles, 'roids
10 Greg/Richard. Shrinker ammo, chaingun (Greg), RPG (Richard)
11 James/Dirk. Freezer ammo, Devastator ammo, jet pack (James), shotgun (Dirk)
12 Chuck/Steve. RPG ammo, chaingun ammo, laser tripbomb (Chuck), Shrinker (Steve)
13 Todd/Allen. Blue key lock. Shotgun ammo, pipebombs, Devastator (Todd), Freezethrower (Allen)
14 Medkits (in pile-drivers), armor, Healing Atoms, Holoduke, laser tripbomb, iris buttons
15 RPG, Devastator
16 Waves. Behind the dancing girl: RPG ammo, Devastator ammo (takes you to 17). In front of the dancing girl: Chaingun ammo, Shrinker ammo (takes you to 18).
17 Healing Atom (looks into 6)
18 Healing Atom, armor (looks into 2)

CHAPTER 8
EDITING GAME PARAMETERS AND SOUNDS EFFECTS

This must be your lucky day, because in addition to all the other great stuff in this book, you also get this bonus chapter torn straight from the pages of the *Duke Nukem 3D Construction Kit: Unauthorized*, also available from Prima Publishing (see the end of the book for ordering information).

Great, you say, but what can I learn from one lousy chapter? Actually, you can learn quite a lot. The first part of this chapter explains how to edit *Duke Nukem*'s configuration (.con) files to create all sort of cool effects–like a pistol that does more damage than the RPG, or bad guys that fall over dead after a single kick from Duke's combat-booted foot. How about a supercharged Duke that runs like he's permanently on Steroids? It's all right here.

The second part shows you how to edit *Duke Nukem 3D*'s sound effects. If you want to replace Duke's familiar comments with quotes from your favorite television show, or wildlife sounds, or even your own voice, go right ahead! You'll learn how to do it in the following pages.

And now, without further ado, let's start hacking.

EDITING CONFIGURATION (CON) FILES

After you install *Duke Nukem 3D* on your hard drive, go look in the directory where Duke was placed. Inside that directory you'll find three files with an extension of .con: defs.con, user.con, and game.con. These three files contain important information on how *Duke Nukem 3D* works. By altering the contents of the .con files, you can make huge changes in *Duke Nukem 3D*. You can adjust the toughness ("hit points") of monsters, the amount of damage each weapon does, or even the speed and durability of Duke himself.

Lots of stuff in these .con files is meaningless to the non-programmer, and it takes quite a while to explain it. Therefore, this chapter will only concern itself with the easiest-to-understand material. If you have some experience with programming, then you will undoubtedly be able to do even more with the .con files than I'm going to show you here.

What good is it to modify .con files? There are two principal reasons. First, you can modify the files for your own personal amusement. For example, it's fun to give all the monsters one lousy hit point and then mow 'em down with single pistol shots. Altered .con files are great in Dukematch, too: if all players use the same modified .con files, you can drastically alter the game environment. Maybe you're sick of everyone stocking up on health? That's easy, just modify everyone's files so that Duke's maximum health is 80 instead of 200.

Note

In many versions of Duke Nukem 3D, Dukematch games automatically use internal .con files instead of the external ones that we'll be looking at and modifying in this chapter. To use altered (external) .con files in Dukematch, everyone must start the Dukematch with the -o command-line option. Therefore, instead of launching your network game by typing:

SETUP [Enter]
or
COMMIT [Enter]

you'd type:

SETUP -O (Enter)
or
COMMIT -O (Enter)

Also, if you are playing Dukematch with modified .con files, everyone must have identical files or the game will crash. In other words, if one person's .con files are modified, then everyone else's must be modified as well, and in exactly the same way.

The other reason to alter these files is to create a specific environment for your levels. When you distribute your levels for others to play, you can also distribute the altered .con files and a note that instructs players to use these files whenever they play your level.

Note

Before you even look at the .con files, you should back up these files in another directory. Make a new directory on your hard disk and call it CON or CONS, then copy defs.con, user.con, and game.con into that directory. That way, after you play around with these files and forget what the original settings were, you can just copy the untouched versions from the CON directory back to the DUKE3D directory.

If you mess up your .con files but forgot to make backups, you might have to re-install **Duke Nukem 3D** on your computer. Furthermore, neither 3D Realms nor anyone else will help you troubleshoot problems with these files, so just remember: once you start to modify those files, you're on your own. That's not to say that you should avoid modifying the files. If you can handle re-installing the game (in a worst-case scenario) then you should have no problems with this section of the book. And if you backup those .con files, you'll never have to re-install the game.

THE DEFS.CON FILE

We won't be discussing the defs.con file in much depth, because that isn't where the neatest stuff happens to be. However, just in case you try some advanced file editing, it's good to know what's in here.

Open up the defs.con file with a text editor such as WordPad in Windows 95 or the Edit command in DOS. With the Edit command, you'd open the file like this:

edit defs.con [Enter]

Inside you'll find a big, sequential list that looks like this:

```
define SECTOREFFECTOR 1
define ACTIVATOR 2
define TOUCHPLATE 3
define ACTIVATORLOCKED 4
define MUSICANDSFX 5
```

This list keeps going and going...but what's the point? In effect, defs.con is a file full of shorthand. The define statements associate names with numbers, and this in turn makes the programmer's job easier. When writing actor code, the programmer can simply write TOUCHPLATE instead of having to remember that the touchplate is object number 3.

Without define statements, the programmer would have to keep all sorts of numbers in his head. Let's say he wants a piece of code that says: "When DUKE gets too CLOSE to the TOUCHPLATE, there's a big EXPLOSION." Instead of writing a bunch of numbers, the code would look something like this:

IF_DUKE CLOSE TOUCHPLATE SMACKPLAYER

Note that these are not actual game definitions, they're just an example of how define statements work. However, some of the actual definitions look very similar to these statements; for example, one routine that injures the player is actually called WACKPLAYER.

Now that you have a working idea of what defs.con is for, let's move right along to the next .con file. There isn't much point in messing around with defs.con unless you're going to rewrite a significant portion of the game.

EDITING THE USER.CON FILE

The user.con file contains several statements that are fun and easy to manipulate. By poking around in this file you'll be able to effect a wide variety of changes on the game. Let's take a look at a few of the best!

Editing Duke's Health

When you open up the user.con file, the first thing you'll notice is a long list of notes from the programmer. These notes are ignored by Duke Nukem because they're bracketed by the symbols /* and */.

Note

The symbol /* tells **Duke Nukem 3D** to ignore everything that appears thereafter. The symbol */ tells the program to start paying attention once again. Large notes from the programmer are usually bracketed by these two symbols. If you want to make your own notes in the .con files, feel free to do so: but make sure they're encased by the /* */ symbols, or else the program will think they're code and try to interpret them, resulting in a crash.

The // symbol also can be used for inserting notes in the .con files. When you place the // symbol at the beginning of a line, you are telling the program to ignore that line completely. You don't need to end your note with another symbol; the note automatically stops at the end of the line.

After the notes comes a section entitles Miscellaneous Game Settings. There are all sorts of fun things to modify in here. To edit Duke's health, look for these two lines:

```
define MAXPLAYERHEALTH 100
define MAXPLAYERATOMICHEALTH 200 // doubles as maxarmor.
```

The first line shows Duke's maximum health without using Healing Atoms. This is also the amount of health Duke starts the game with. So if you change the number from 100 to 800 and save the file, Duke starts the game with 800 health. As you might expect, this has profound repercussions on gameplay.

The second line shows Duke's maximum "Atomic Health", which is the maximum amount of health he can get as a result of picking up Healing Atoms. Change the number if you'd like: by changing it to 100, you can make Healing Atoms much less useful and make Dukematch a lot quicker and bloodier.

Long-Armed Duke
(Editing Retrieval Distance)

Though this is more of a silly modification than anything else, you can enable Duke to pick up items without even getting close by increasing the number in this line:

```
define RETRIEVEDISTANCE 844
```

Triple or quadruple this number and Duke will find himself grabbing things that aren't anywhere near him! He will even get stuff that's behind walls and completely out of sight.

Pinball Duke (Editing Duke's Speed)

Also in the Miscellaneous Game Settings section is a line that looks like this:

```
define RUNNINGSPEED 53200
```

This number states how fast Duke can run. Actually, it doesn't adjust his speed so much as his friction: the higher the number, the less friction Duke has. That means that when you make the number higher, Duke not only gets faster but he becomes harder to control because he won't stop running when you let go of the keys: he'll keep sliding along, bouncing off walls and coasting over small obstacles.

Change the number to 73200 and Duke will run so fast that he flies off the edge of the game world and causes a game error. Try it! A speed of 63200 won't cause the game to crash, but it makes Duke incredibly fast and difficult to control. This might be a fun setting for a Dukematch session. Remember, though: everyone must have the exact same changes to their user.con file or Dukematch won't work.

Changing Maximum Ammo Amounts and Ammo Rewards

Another fun item under Miscellaneous Game Settings is a set of maximum ammunition values. These numbers determine how much ammunition Duke can hold for any given weapon at once. The values look like this:

```
define MAXPISTOLAMMO 200
define MAXSHOTGUNAMMO 50
define MAXCHAINGUNAMMO 200
define MAXRPGAMMO 50
```

The first line, for example, states that Duke can only carry around 200 bullets for the pistol at any given time. If you were to change the number to 2000 instead of 200, then Duke would be able to carry 2000 bullets at once.

Later in the user.con file is another paragraph of ammunition-related items. Here are a few lines from that one:

```
define PISTOLAMMOAMOUNT 12
define SHOTGUNAMMOAMOUNT 10
define CHAINGUNAMMOAMOUNT 50
define RPGAMMOBOX 5
```

These lines don't affect the amount of ammunition Duke can hold–rather, they affect how much ammunition Duke gets when he picks up specific ammunition items. For example, the RPGAMMOBOX line defines how many rockets Duke receives when he walks across a box of RPG ammunition. By cranking up this value to 50, you could make the game much easier, since Duke would get tons of rockets from every box of RPG ammo he discovers.

In Dukematch, extra ammunition just tends to make things even more insane. Increase the maximum RPG ammo value to 500 and the RPGAMMOBOX value to 500 as well, and end up with players toting around virtually limitless supplies of rockets. Players will start shooting randomly into dark corners and into common hiding places, simply hoping to get a cheap shot–after all, with that much ammunition there's very little to lose by firing indiscriminately.

Modifying Blast Radii

Somewhat farther down, you'll find a section labeled "Various blasting radius distances." These entries all look like this:

```
define RPGBLASTRADIU 1780
define PIPEBOMBRADIUS 2500
```

By changing the numbers you can give these weapons a greater or lesser blast radius. A pipe bomb blast radius of 10000, for example, would make the bomb incredibly nasty in Dukematch—players couldn't just run back a few paces to get out of its range. Of course, this is a double-edged sword. You couldn't simply lob pipe bombs at nearby opponents and detonate them immediately, because you would certainly be caught in the blast as well. Instead, you'd have to run behind a corner before detonating the bomb.

Adjusting Weapon Strengths

One of the most fun and easy things to modify in *Duke Nukem 3D* is weapon strength. These values appear in a section labeled, appropriately enough, Weapon Strengths. The first few entries look like this:

```
// Weapon Strengths

define KNEE_WEAPON_STRENGTH 10
define PISTOL_WEAPON_STRENGTH 6 //
Adds rand()%5 (0 to 5)
define HANDBOMB_WEAPON_STRENGTH 140
```

You can have tremendous good fun just by setting KNEE_WEAPON_STRENGTH at 100. That makes Duke's weak kicking attack almost as powerful as an RPG launcher or a pipe bomb, drastically altering the dynamics of Dukematch. This way, even a completely unarmed player is positively lethal!

Weapon strength doesn't just affect how much damage a weapon does, it also affects how much your target gets pushed around when hit by that weapon. To see this principle in action, change the pistol's strength to 200 and load up the game. Run up to a monster—any monster—and shoot them once with the pistol. Note that they don't just die on the spot; they get blasted backwards about 10 to 20 feet as well. The effect can be quite comical. I have played through a few game levels with the pistol adjusted this way, and found it to be a great stress-reliever. Nothing conveys such a sense of power as a weapon that not only destroys enemies outright, but tosses them around like rag dolls as well.

Editing Monster Hit Points

Another fun thing to do is edit monster's hit points, making them ultra-tough or incredibly weak. Monster hit points are clearly labeled in the user.con file, and appear like this:

```
// Enemy strengths (hit points).
define TROOPSTRENGTH 30
define PIGCOPSTRENGTH 100
```

You could make Dukematch a lot more challenging by toughening up the monsters—give PigCops 200 hit points instead of 100, and the Assault Troopers 80 hit points instead of 30. This makes creatures a legitimate hazard in Dukematch, and makes the non-human threat almost as dangerous as the human players.

Alternately, you could change every creature's hit points to 1 and treat the game as a no-stress shooting gallery. Just shoot 'em with a weapon—any weapon will do—and watch 'em fall.

Editing Game Messages

Though in-game messages don't actually affect the mechanics of *Duke Nukem 3D*, they definitely affect the flavor of the game. You can either customize these messages to your personal tastes for your own enjoyment, or modify them to add flavor to your custom-made levels.

The game messages look like this:

```
// Maximum quote size is 64 characters.
definequote  0  AUTO AIMING
definequote  1  MANUAL AIMING / SNIPER MODE!
definequote  2  ACTIVATED
definequote  3  MEDKIT
```

To change the messages, simply delete the text and type in your own. Remember, though: just as the warning message says, your quote cannot be longer than 64 characters.

Why would you want to change these quotes? Well, let's say that you created a medieval-theme level and planned to distribute edited .con files along with it. You could change the game messages to reflect the theme of your level. For example, look at definequote 3, shown above. This is the message that tells Duke he's got a Medkit. In your altered .con files, you could change this from Medkit to Healing Herbs or Elixir of Life. Even without changing the actual appearance of the Medkit, you've added some medieval flavor to your level just by changing the quote. And if you do manage to change the actual appearance of the object, so much the better. There's more on that in the *Duke Nukem 3D Construction Kit: Unauthorized*.

Altering Level Names and Parameters

One of the best uses for an edited .con file is changing level names. If you go through all the trouble of creating a great original game level, there's no reason why it should be labeled Hollywood Holocaust or Red Light District when players attempt to boot it up. Give it your own name instead!

Level names and information appear like this:

```
definelevelname 0 0 E1L1.map 01:45 00:53
HOLLYWOOD HOLOCAUST
definelevelname 0 1 E1L2.map 05:10 03:21
RED LIGHT DISTRICT
```

In the Hollywood Holocaust line, the numbers are as follows:

- ► E1L1.map simply means that this is Episode 1, Level 1 of the game. This part should not be altered.

- 01:45 is the par time for the level, 1 minute and 45 seconds. Feel free to change this number for your own custom-made levels.

- 00:53 is the 3D Realms par time, which is just a really tough par time to beat. You can alter this as well.

- HOLLYWOOD HOLOCAUST is the level title, which is what many people will want to change. By changing the text to read MY LEVEL or DISCO INFERNO or something similar, you effectively re-name the level. The new level name is displayed whenever the player enters that level, and appears on the auto-map of that level as well.

EDITING THE GAME.CON FILE

We aren't going to go into much detail about game.con. This is not because editing game.con would be pointless[em]far from it! You can make all sorts of strange and fantastic things happen when you edit game.con. The problem is that editing game.con can be a complicated and troublesome affair unless you happen to be a programmer. Even veteran hackers on the Internet tend to have problems with it.

What does game.con contain? Well, first of all, it includes some brief instructions for Duke Nukem 3D about how to get everything started: for example, it tells the game to load up defs.con and user.con. The vast majority of this file, however, is actor code. All objects, creatures and items in Duke Nukem 3D–in other words, everything except the architecture–are referred to as actors. This file tells the game engine how each actor behaves. For example, let's look at a really simple actor: fire. You remember the burning dumpster in the street in Hollywood Holocaust? Well, how do you think those flames got there? Fire is an actor, just like every other piece of scenery is an actor, so the level designer just put an object labeled Fire on the map–and there it was.

Here's some FIRE code:

```
actor BURNING WEAK BURNING_FLAME
state burningstate
enda
```

```
actor BURNING2 WEAK BURNING_FLAME
state burningstate
end
```

Basically, this code is just telling the game which sprites are displayed when the fire is burning, and that the fire does a little damage to Duke.

EDITING GAME SOUNDS

It's fun to add different sound to *Duke Nukem 3D*. Some players add different sounds just for their own enjoyment, because it adds variety to the game. However, you can also include custom sounds in a ZIP file with your homemade levels, thus ensuring that everyone who plays your level can experience your new sound effects as well.

Editing game sounds is a lot easier than you might think. When *Duke Nukem 3D* first starts up, it automatically loads the basic sound effects contained in the huge duke3d.grp file. However, before it loads those default sounds, it first looks in the DUKE3D directory for other sounds. Any sound effects sitting in that directory will override the basic sounds. It's just a matter of giving the new sound effect the same name as the sound effect you'd like to replace.

Here's a few facts about sound effects in *Duke Nukem 3D*.

- In theory, *Duke Nukem 3D* accepts sounds in either the .voc or .wav file format. In practice, I find that the .voc format seems to work best.

- *Duke Nukem 3D* doesn't come with any sound effects utilities, so it's up to you to find a program that let you record sounds in the .voc or .wav formats, or convert sounds to those formats. Optionally, you can scrounge around on the Internet for sounds—and the sounds you find are likely to be in those formats. Appendix A of the *Duke Nukem 3D Construction Kit: Unauthorized* gives a list of useful Internet sites.

- There are about 250 sounds in *Duke Nukem 3D*. The end of this section tells you where to find the full list.

☞ The second half of the user.con file (see above) is called Actor Sounds, and it's a big list of situations and the sound effects that that play in those situations.

LOOKING UP SOUND EFFECTS IN USER.CON

How should you interpret the list of sound effects found in Actor Sounds, the second half of user.con? Let's take a look at a few examples.

The first line in the Actor Sounds section looks like this:

definesound PRED_ROAM roam06.voc 0 0 3 0 0

PRED_ROAM means that this is the sound effect Duke hears when the Assault Trooper (often called the Predator Trooper) is ROAMing around. Looking to the right, we see several numbers. As explained in the text preceding the Actor Sounds section, these numbers are technical parameters, and in most cases you don't want to change them. The first two numbers define a range of random pitch variations, the third number is a priority flag, the fourth number is a technical variable, and the fifth number is a volume adjustment. That's not what you're interested in; you probably want to leave those alone!

What you are interested in, however, is the .voc file: roam06.voc. That's the "Assault Trooper Roaming Around" sound. If you wanted to change that sound effect, you'd make a note of the name and follow the procedure outlined in Quick and Easy Sound Replacement, below.

Here's another example:

definesound CHAINGUN_FIRE chaingun.voc
-204-204 254 0 512

This one isn't too hard to figure out. CHAINGUN_FIRE means it's the sound that the chaingun (otherwise known as the ripper) makes when it's being fired. Looking to the right, we see that the chaingun firing noise is chaingun.voc.

Now you know how to look in user.con and figure out the names of sound effects. Here's how to put that knowledge to good use.

QUICK AND EASY SOUND REPLACEMENT

This quick process will help you replace sound effects in *Duke Nukem 3D*.

1. Look in user.con for the sound effect you want to replace. In this case, let's say you want to replace the "pistol firing" sound. We find the appropriate line in user.con:

   definesound PISTOL_FIRE pistol.voc-64 0 254 00

2. Create or locate the new sound you want to use, making sure it's in .voc format. (Remember, the .wav format supposedly works too, but it can be problematic.) For our example, let's say it's a sound of a dog barking, called bark.voc

3. Rename the new sound so it shares the same name as the default sound. In this case, we'd type this at the DOS prompt:

   rename bark.voc pistol.voc [Enter]

4. Move the newly renamed file into the DUKE3D directory if it isn't there already.

That's all! Your custom-made pistol noise will now play in the game. In this example, we'd hear a barking noise every time Duke fired the pistol.

To return to the default pistol sound effect, I could simply move pistol.voc out of the DUKE3D directory, or delete it. In its absence, the program will use the default pistol noise, which is safely stored in the DUKE3D.GRP file.

Note

In this example we changed the new sound's filename (bark.voc) so that it shared the default pistol sound filename (pistol.voc). Instead, we could have gone into user.con and changed the pistol sound line from this:

definesound PISTOL_FIRE pistol.voc-64 0 254 00

to this:

definesound PISTOL_FIRE bark.voc-64 0 254 00

In other words, you can either change the new sound's filename to match the filename listed in user.con, or you can change the filename in user.con to match your new sound's filename. I suggest you stick to changing the new filename, like we did in the example. It's easier and you don't run the risk of messing up your user.con file.

FINDING THE SOUNDS LIST

All right, now you know how to add your own sound effects—but when you're using BUILD and you want to place a MUSICANDSFX sprite, how do you know what number equates with what sound? Easy! The defs.con file has a list of every sound used in *Duke Nukem 3D*. This list appears toward the end of the defs.con file, and it starts out like this:

```
define KICK_HIT 0
define PISTOL_RICOCHET 1
define PISTOL_BODYHIT 2
define PISTOL_FIRE 3
```

Print out this list, and whenever you want to place a sound effect, you can look to this list for the appropriate sound number. This is where you'll find that sounds number 1 through 5 are pistol noises, sounds 165 through 167 are good door noises, and so forth. Be warned that some sounds won't work in some situations. The only way to discover which sounds are usable is through trial and error.

THAT'S ALL, FOLKS!

If you're interested in learning how to build your own game levels or import your own graphics into *Duke Nukem 3D*, be sure to check out the full version of the *Duke Nukem 3D Construction Kit: Unauthorized*.

You already have the all tools to build new game levels–in fact, they're sitting right there on your *Duke Nukem 3D* CD-ROM. However, while these building tools are extremely powerful, their documentation is woefully incomplete. The *Duke Nukem 3D Construction Kit: Unauthorized* gives you all the information you need to start building your own game levels, and even walks you step-by-step through the creation of a simple map. Later chapters deal with advanced effects like breakable glass windows, collapsing bridges, moving elevators, and subway trains with multiple stops. The possibilities are virtually limitless, so get your copy and start building today!

APPENDIX
SECRET MISSIONS

The Secret Missions in *Duke Nukem* are some of the most entertaining thrill rides in the entire game, but they are also generally set apart from the rest of the game by a certain sense of style—a code of game conduct unlike the other "regular" missions.

With the exception of the last Secret Mission (Freeway), all bear little resemblance to the standard Duke missions. The first three Secrets—Spin Cycle, Lunatic Fringe and Tier Drops—contain large numbers of weapons and monsters in small spaces. For that reason, we recommend that you save the game to a separate slot before venturing to those three: the odds of coming out with a net gain over the health and supplies you begin with is really a crap shoot.

The missions in this section are accessible without the warp code through Secret Mission switches in four places in Episodes Two and Three. In Episode Two, the missions with Secret Mission switches are Mission 5: Occupied Territory and Mission 8: Dark Side. In Episode Three, look for switches in Mission 5: Movie Set and in Mission 8: Motel Hell.

Note also that for one mission in this section, Lunatic Fringe, we decided that a map wasn't really that helpful. Play it, and find out why.

SECRET MISSION: SPIN CYCLE

This mission is pure rollickin' Duke fun. You may or may not come out ahead of the game with regard to weapons and ammo, however, so it is best to consider this an amusing bonus, but not really part of the grand Duke scheme of things.

The premise is simple: plenty of monsters and mayhem on a large, revolving floorway. A central hub and outer area remain fixed and relative to one another, while the Duke opens doors, unleashing baddies and claiming prizes.

Throwing the switches in the outer stations opens and unlocks doors on the central hub, and there are four such stations. Once all the outer station switches have been tripped, throwing the switches in the four hub rooms opens up the central hub area. You guessed it: more goodies, more baddies.

Of course, if you take this level seriously, and practice your aim with regard to the unique spinning environment, you can wreak all kinds of hell. For pure visceral impact, you might try opening all the hub rooms in rapid succession, without pausing to fight any of the new arrivals. Now *that's* a party.

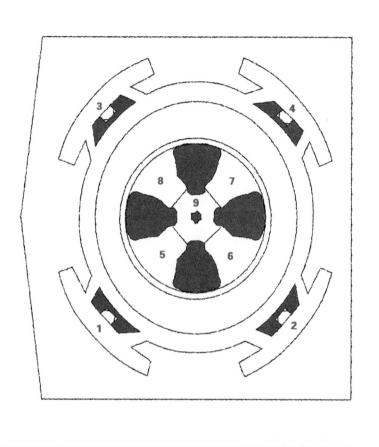

Legend
Secret Place   Wall   Sub-level

HIGHLIGHTS

- Spinning circular floorway
- Intriguing artillery trajectories
- Combat in a crowd

SECRET LEVEL: SPIN CYCLE AT-A-GLANCE

1 Alpha Station: shotgun, pipebombs, chaingun ammo, Devastator ammo, portable medkit

2 Delta Station: RPG ammo, chaingun ammo, Healing Atom, Shrinker, shotgun, medkit

3 Beta Station: RPG ammo, chaingun ammo, Healing Atom, pistol, shotgun ammo

4 Gamma Station: chaingun ammo, Devastator ammo, portable medkit, shotgun shells

5 Across from Alpha Station: Armor, pistol ammo, chaingun

6 Across from Delta Station: RPG cannon, Shrinker ammo

7 Across from Gamma Station: Freezethrower, Freezethrower ammo, night vision goggles, pistol ammo

8 Across from Beta Station: shotgun ammo, portable medkit, Shrinker

9 Holoduke, Devastator, End

The Duke of Twirl

1 You enter the Spin Cycle near Alpha Station. Nearby you'll acquire a shotgun and pipebombs, while through the door waits a stash of ammo for both the chaingun and the Devastator, as well as a portable medkit.

2 Inside Delta Station are RPG and chaingun ammo, with a Healing Atom as a special added bonus. Outside in the hallway are a Shrinker, shotgun, and large medkit.

3 Inside Beta Station are loads of ammo for both RPG and chaingun, as well as a Healing Atom. A pistol and shotgun ammo lie in the hallway outside.

4 Inside Gamma Station: more ammo for the chaingun and the Devastator, and another portable medkit. On the floor outside is a measly box of shotgun shells.

5 In the center hub across from Alpha Station are Armor and pistol ammo. Party down. A chaingun lies out front.

6 In front of the door across from Delta Station lies an RPG cannon. Inside is ammo for the Shrinker.

7 In front of the door across from Gamma Station rests a Freezethrower. Inside are Freezethrower ammo, night vision goggles, and pistol ammo.

8 In the center hub room across from Beta Station are shotgun shells and a portable medkit. Out front is a Shrinker.

9 Two big boss apes appear when you set foot in the center room of the hub. The good news is that they're sissies by Duke standards—six RPG shots apiece nets you Holoduke and a Devastator.

SECRET MISSION: LUNATIC FRINGE

Throw the switch behind you as the mission begins, and test the Lunatic Fringe.

The perimeter is guarded by Aliens and Enforcers, while inside the hub are three Boss Monsters soon to be screaming for your blood. A fourth appears when you enter the center of the hub, near the Healing Atoms.

Shooting the switches near the chicks opens the hub. The chicks themselves can only be killed with heavy artillery, and their unpleasant demise invites more Alien scum to the party. The big trick to this mission—there are many small tricks—is knowing that once you kill the boss monsters, the rest of the local scumbags seem to quit respawning.

First: kill the babes, and take care of the Aliens that arrive. Shoot both switches near the chicks and then circle right. When you make the 360: more chicks, more switches. Shooting the last switch opens a large door in the hub behind you. From that position, as you face the hub, a Boss Monster is in the window to your right, just out of view. Kill him with heavy weaponry. Inside, through the large door, are two more Boss Monsters on the floor level. By standing on the walkway you can easily dispatch them with pipebombs. Just lure them over directly beneath you, where they can't return fire, and bombs away. Using the center of the hub as a backboard works quite nicely.

When you enter the center of the hub, near the Healing Atoms and freezer ammo, the fourth and final Boss Monster will start to patrol the perimeter. Bait him inside the building, and kill him as you did the last two.

As the battle is ongoing, you'll occasionally be jumped by Aliens or Enforcers. Since the Enforcers can't fly, they usually wind up in the same predicament as their bosses—playing center fielder to the cruelest pop fly. Use the chaingun on the lesser beings—that's the one thing this mission never runs out of.

Everything in the way of ammo and supplies is here in abundance, with the notable exception of a jet pack. Being frugal with your firepower is the key to coming back from the Fringe with enough stuff to get you through the final mission in Episode Two.

A switch inside the hub—one of those Alien hand print deals, facing the center of the hub inside the largest bay window—opens the exit door. It'll appear in the wall area where you came in after you circle the hub. Let the shrink ray hit you, and proceed to the end-of-the-level switch.

Then thank your lucky stars, Lunar Duke, that you saved the game before venturing to the Lunatic Fringe.

SECRET MISSION: TIER DROPS

Now this is a Secret Mission. Plenty of combat, loads of goodies, and even a triple Boss Monster execution. It may be that the Secret Missions in Episode Two soured you on the concept: they seemed to cost you more than you could ever hope to gain in terms of supplies and ammunition. Not so with Tier Drops. Play your cards right, and you may actually leave the mission in better shape than when you started off. What a concept.

Basically, Tier Drops is a square hallway that flanks four different encounter areas—one of those perception tricks that would make David Copperfield envious. At the corners of the square are raised platforms.

Within each chamber are different collections of monsters and Nukem party favors. The chambers also interconnect through vertical tunnels, though that's not really a prudent mode of travel when you're thinking about dropping into the corner of a room full of scum.

This is fun stuff, and destined to become an all-time classic Dukematch mission.

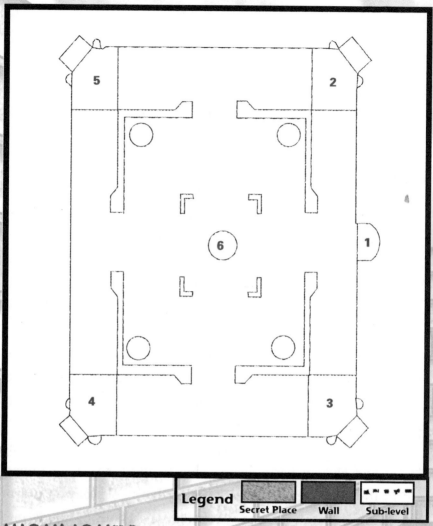

Legend — Secret Place — Wall — Sub-level

HIGHLIGHTS

- Four secret places
- A chance to completely stock up
- (With the exception of a scuba tank...)

Secret Mission: Tier Drops At-a-Glance

1 Medkits

2 Alpha corner: steroids, Armor, pistol ammo, shotgun ammo, Devastator ammo

3 Beta corner: night vision goggles, portable medkit, chaingun ammo, Shrinker ammo, shotgun

4 Gamma corner: medkits, jet pack, RPG ammo, shotgun ammo

5 Delta corner: Holoduke, laser tripbombs, pipebombs, Freezethrower ammo, pistol

6 Main encounter area

TIERS OF JOY

1   Behind you as the mission begins are three large medkits. Just in case.

> **Tip**
>
> The computer panels in each corner section slide to reveal items, and the wall between each panel separates to reveal Secret Places brimming with Nukem treasures.

2   Alpha corner: steroids and Armor in side panels; pistol ammo, shotgun and Devastator ammo in the central chamber.

3   Beta: night vision goggles and a portable medkit in the side panels; chaingun ammo, Shrinker ammo, and a shotgun in the central chamber.

4   Gamma: large medkits and a jet pack in the side panels; RPG ammo and shotgun shells in the central chamber.

5   Delta: Holoduke and three laser tripbombs in side panels, pipe-bombs, Freezethrower ammo, and pistol in central chamber.

6   The four encounter areas, in our recommended order of disposal:

   ☞   The room accessible between Alpha and Beta corners is inhabited by Aliens. Scattered about you'll find ammo for the chaingun and freezer, as well as a Shrinker.

   ☞   The area between Delta and Gamma is the province of Octabrains. Yes, no matter how many of them there are, you can believe none of them has ever seen Holoduke before.... Once they've been properly introduced, you can collect shotgun ammo, a chaingun, and several large medkits.

   ☞   The real test lies between the corners of Alpha and Delta. The central construct is full of pods and guarded by

Assault Commanders, and Pig Cops ring the perimeter. When you engage, which you should do with the Devastator—rake the gazebo to clean the pods and stir things up—three Boss Monsters join the fray. The Bosses, however, commit a major tactical blunder in that they'll follow you into the corridor, where you can hop up on a corner piece and suddenly be out of their line of fire. Three Boss Monsters: point blank execution. How sweet it is.

Assuming you did a good job on the pods up front, now all you have to deal with are a handful of Assault Commanders and the occasional straggler Pig Cop. Once the coast is clear, you're free to load up on goodies, including two RPG cannons, a Devastator, many boxes of ammo for both RPG and Devastator, shotgun shells aplenty, and Healing Atoms.

☞ Assault Commanders rule between Gamma and Beta corners, an area littered with chaingun ammo and large medkits. There's also a Devastator and a box of RPG ammo all by their lonesome. Inside the central chamber is a Boss Monster, a Freezer and the end-of-the-level switch, as well as three juicy Healing Atoms.

SECRET MISSION: FREEWAY

This is the oddball of the Secret Missions—a mission that just as easily could have been part of the regular game missions. No weird perception tricks or endless supplies of ammo and monsters, Freeways is a freebie: an actual straight-up Duke mission, and a pretty cool one at that.

From here, you go to the big showdown, and there's no shortage of ammo on the final field of battle, so don't be afraid to cut loose a little. It'll be awhile before you see a Pig Cop eat an RPG again.

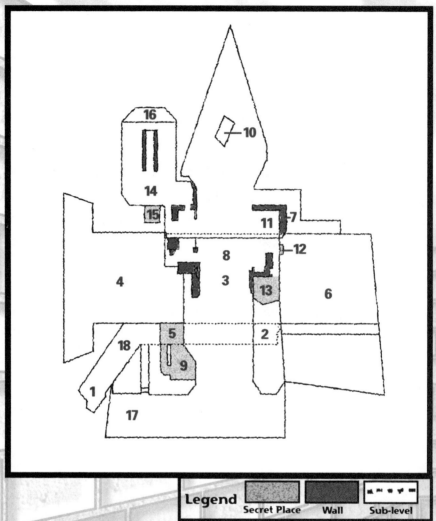

Legend

Secret Place	Wall	Sub-level

HIGHLIGHTS

- Five secret places
- Possible scum Termination
- Sideways skyscraper

Secret Mission: Freeway At-a-Glance

1 Shotgun, shotgun ammo, Healing Atom, RPG ammo, RPG
2 Armor, laser trip bombs, pistol ammo, medkit
3 Devastator, Healing Atom
4 Medkits, shotgun, shotgun ammo, steroids,
   Devastator ammo, portable medkit
* 5 Freezethrower
6 Shotgun ammo, Freezethrower ammo, large medkit, RPG ammo,
   night vision goggles
7 Medkit, shotgun ammo
8 Devastator ammo, portable medkit, pipebombs, steroids,
   small medkits, armor
* 9 Devastator ammo, Shrinker
*10 Shotgun ammo, medkit, jet pack
11 Pipebombs, medkit, shotgun ammo, blue key, Devastator ammo
*12 Freezethrower ammo, chaingun
13 Healing Atoms
14 RPG ammo, chaingun ammo, RPG
*15 Pipebombs, armor
16 Red key, Freezethrower, medkit
17 Red key lock, medkit
18 Medkit, End

*Denotes secret place

ROAD KILL

1   Clear the underwater area of Octabrains. Below, where the mission began, are a shotgun and ammo, as well as a weak spot in the wall. The proper firepower applied to the crack yields a Healing Atom and RPG ammo. At the far end of the underwater area lies an RPG cannon, and a prudent Duke will swim back to the grating with the opening in it before popping topside.

2   Drones patrol the area above water, and once you climb out to grab the nearby Armor, laser trip bombs, pistol ammo, and small medkit, you'll begin to draw all kinds of unwanted attention. Battling from the tunnel is a no-win proposition: time to bust outta here, using the weak spot in the wall that's just to the right of the support column.

3   In the tunnel outside waits a big bunch of nastiness. Pig Cops in recon vehicles, Pig Cops lurking in the shadows, at least one Drone. Stand in the opening you've created and activate the night vision goggles briefly, just so you can see everyone who's gunning for you.
    Your first priority should be the nearby Pig Cops on foot, since you can't afford to let them stand and blast away. The recon vehicles will stop and hover nearby to get in their licks, and you should deal with them as quickly as possible. Once the recon vehicles and the Drone have been disposed of, go stand near one of the central columns between lanes. That'll make it much harder for foes in the street outside to target you.
    When the panic has subsided, grab up the Devastator and the Healing Atom (in the trashcan).

4   Tend to the Pig Cops in the outside area—for reference sake, the area to your left as you exited the sewer. Use the support columns for cover, and make sure you check both sides of the street before venturing out into daylight. On the central divider rests a pair of small medkits. Use the trashcans to reach the ledges before you blow them open to discover a shotgun and shotgun ammo.
    On one ledge is a refill of 'roids and some Devastator ammo, while on the other sits a portable medkit. Work your way along the ledge on the side where you found the portable medkit, and discover a secret place.

5   Secret place. The last window on the ledge opens to reveal a room with a lone Pig Cop, currently guarding a Freezethrower. Relieve him of his duties, and venture to the other side of the underpass.

6   Again, work your way along the walls to get the first shot at the enemies on the ledges above. Take out the Pig Cop on the left, then the three Enforcers that come from the right. More Pig Cops will show up from the left when you start to collect the prizes: shotgun ammo, Freezethrower ammo, a large medkit, and a box of shells for the RPG. There's also night vision goggles in the area where the Enforcers came from.

7   When you move towards the large medkit in the direction of the street outside, a series of explosions rips through the area. Once things start shaking, retreat until the blasts have subsided, then return and kill the lone surviving Pig Cop. On the other side of the flames you'll pick up more shotgun ammo.

8   Approach the street with caution. There's a Boss Monster at the far end, and you don't want to get his attention right away. Peek just out of the alley and two Enforcers will dive out of the windows in front of you. Dispatch them, then leap out and unload about 40 rounds of Devastator at the big space monkey.
    A flock of Drones tries to sneak up behind you as you walk the street, so be ready. If you run over and grab the Devastator ammo from the alley, and sprint along that wall to where the two Pig Cops are stationed near the blue key lock, you can kill them, then return to the street for the Drones. Use the freeway as a big oval, and put distance between you and the Drones before turning and firing.
    A word of caution: there's no need to go near Car 54 just yet. That area aside, you can clean the street of the aforementioned Devastator ammo, and also a portable medkit, pipebombs, steroids, two small medkits, and armor. Check the window in the wall nearest the blue key lock to discover a secret place.

9   Secret place. Inside a cozy little apartment are a trio of Enforcers (one lurks on the stairs) and also ammo for the Devastator and a Shrinker. Blowing the weak spot at the top of the stairs reveals another route to room (4).

10 Secret place. If you explore the toppled building at one end of the street, you'll find a hole in the middle, and a room with a pair of Enforcers. There's also shotgun shells (one box inside; one on the buildings face) a large medkit, and also a jet pack.... Time to put it to use.

11 Jet pack up to the room where the Enforcers have gathered, and hammer them into submission. Inside you'll discover pipebombs, a small medkit, shotgun shells and the blue key. The bookcase conceals a compartment holding two boxes of ammo for the Devastator. Before you go, blow the weak spot in the door to uncover a secret place.

12 Secret place. A trio of pods provides little protection for the freezer ammo and chaingun (behind the flames). Check the monitor, then go put that blue key in the lock.

13 If you take the Healing Atoms from the ledge outside, a pair of Boss Monsters show up to rain on your parade. Feel free to liberally dispense Devastator ammo—past these guys, you'll no longer have much of a need for it.

14 Using the blue key on the lock across the street opens an elevator with a Pig Cop passenger. Upstairs, Enforcers and Drones struggle to keep you from two boxes of ammo for the RPG, chaingun ammo, and an RPG cannon. The switch closest to you when you hop off the elevator stops the tracks from moving.

15 Secret place. When you've cleared the machine area of scum, look at the wall facing the machine—the one with the two broad yellow/black stripes on either side of a vertical column. There's a secret place back there, and those stripes are really windows. Firing an RPG or two through the stripes takes care of the two Enforcers, and in addition to whatever they drop, there's a box of pipebombs and an Armor vest that's yours to keep. Just hop through the wall.

16 Now lace the back of the room—near the wall with the hazard stripe around the bottom of it—with pipebombs. The switches to the right or left of the wall open the whole section, and it's full of Enforcers. You figure out the rest. When the smoke has cleared, the red key is yours for the taking, as is a freezer, a large medkit, and whatever ammo might have been coughed up.

17 The red key lock is back on street level, near the overturned Car 54. As you approach the car, a tremendous explosion occurs, and Pig Cops rush out to greet you. Once the introduction has concluded, the large medkit at the back of the alley awaits.

18 Accessing the red key lock opens the door on a couple of Pig Cops and a seemingly dead-end hallway. Shoot the fire extinguisher on the wall, however, and more hall is revealed. Inside are a pair of Octabrain, a large medkit, and the end-of-the-level switch.

PRIMA'S DUKE NUKEM 3D CONSTRUCTION KIT: UNAUTHORIZED

Available Now from Prima Publishing!

You played their game, now design your own! You can't get enough of the non-stop, bloodthirsty action in *Duke Nukem™ 3D*, and you're yearning for more. Don't settle for modifying someone else's levels and monsters—with **Prima's Duke Nukem 3D Construction Kit: Unauthorized** you can construct your own unique levels right down to the art work on the walls!

This book is all you need to construct a superior Nukem challenge. Inside, a master level-builder walks you step-by-step through the process so you can:

•Create entirely new bone-crushing levels
•Spawn diabolical monsters that'll blow your friends away
•Incorporate your own graphics and sound effects
•Build the ultimate Dukematch playground
•And much more!

$19.99
ISBN 0-7615-0710-8
By Joe Grant Bell

Prima Publishing
PO Box 629000, El Dorado Hills, CA 95762
To Order: Call 1-800-531-2343

To Order Books

Please send me the following items:

Quantity	Title	Unit Price	Total
_____	_____	$ _____	$ _____
_____	_____	$ _____	$ _____
_____	_____	$ _____	$ _____
_____	_____	$ _____	$ _____
_____	_____	$ _____	$ _____
_____	_____	$ _____	$ _____

Subtotal	$ _____
7.25% Sales Tax (CA only)	$ _____
8.25% Sales Tax (TN only)	$ _____
5.0% Sales Tax (MD and IN only)	$ _____
7.0% G.S.T. Canadian Orders	$ _____
Shipping and Handling*	$ _____
Total Order	$ _____

Within Domestic U.S. *$5.00 shipping and handling charge for the first book and $.50 for each additional book. Hawaii, Foreign and all Priority Request orders: Call Order Entry department for price quote at 916/632-4400

By Telephone: With MC or Visa, call (916) 632-4400. Mon-Fri, 9-4 PST.
By Mail: Just fill out the information below and send with your remittance to:

Prima Publishing
P.O. Box 1260BK
Rocklin, CA 95677

Satisfaction unconditionally guaranteed.

My name is _____

I live at _____

City_____ State_____ Zip_____

MC/Visa#_____ Exp. _____

Signature_____